Library of
Davidson College

Fundamentals of Pure and Applied Economics 42

Editors in Chief: Jacques Lesourne and Hugo Sonnenschein

Reduced Forms of Rational Expectations Models

Laurence Broze,
Christian Gouriéroux
and Ariane Szafarz

harwood academic publishers

Reduced Forms of Rational Expectations Models

FUNDAMENTALS OF PURE AND APPLIED ECONOMICS

EDITORS IN CHIEF

J. LESOURNE, Conservatoire National des Arts et Métiers, Paris, France

H. SONNENSCHEIN, University of Pennsylvania Philadelphia, PA, USA

ADVISORY BOARD

K. ARROW, Stanford, CA, USA
W. BAUMOL, Princeton, NJ, USA
W. A. LEWIS, Princeton, NJ, USA
S. TSURU, Tokyo, Japan

Fundamentals of Pure and Applied Economics is an international series of titles divided by discipline into sections. A list of sections and their editors and of published titles may be found at the back of this volume.

Reduced Forms of Rational Expectations Models

Laurence Broze
Université de Lille III, France and CORE, Belgium

Christian Gouriéroux
CEPREMAP Paris, France

Ariane Szafarz
Centre d'Economie Mathématique et d'Econométrie de l'Université Libre de Bruxelles, Belgium

A volume in the Macroeconomic Theory section
edited by
Jean-Michel Grandmont
CEPREMAP, Paris, France

harwood academic publishers
chur · london · paris · new york · melbourne

© 1990 by Harwood Academic Publishers GmbH
Poststrasse 22, 7000 Chur, Switzerland
All rights reserved

Harwood Academic Publishers

Post Office Box 197
London WC2E 9PX
United Kingdom

58, rue Lhomond
75005 Paris
France

Post Office Box 786
Cooper Station
New York, New York 10276
United States of America

Private Bag 8
Camberwell, Victoria 3124
Australia

Library of Congress Cataloging-in-Publication Data

Broze, Laurence, 1960-
   Reduced forms of rational expectations models / Laurence Broze, Christian Gouriéroux, and Ariane Szafarz.
     p.   cm. — (Fundamentals of pure and applied economics, ISSN 0191-1708; v. 42. Macroeconomic theory section)
   Includes bibliographical references.
   ISBN 3-7186-5031-2
   1. Rational expectations (Economic theory—Mathematical models. 2. Macroeconomics—Mathematical models. I. Gouriéroux, Christian, 1949- . II. Szafarz, Ariane, 1958- . III. Title. IV. Series: Fundamentals of pure and applied economics; v. 42. V. Series: Fundamentals of pure and applied economics. Macroeconomic theory section.
HB172.5.B774   1990
339′.01′5113—dc20   90-4392
                                                                                                       CIP

No part of this book may be reproduced or utilized in any form or by any means, electronic or mechanical, including photocopying and recording, or any information storage or retrieval system, without permission in writing from the publisher. Printed in the United Kingdom.

Contents

Introduction to the Series	ix
Introduction	1
Plan of the monograph	4
References	6
1. Expectation Schemes	6
1. Expectations	6
1.1. Basic notions	6
1.2. Successive predictions	7
2. Adaptive scheme	8
2.1. The adaptive form	8
2.2. The extrapolative form	11
3. Rational scheme	11
3.1. Optimal predictions	11
3.2. Some properties of optimal predictions	12
3.3. Prediction errors and updating	16
References	19
2. A Model with Current Expectations	20
1. An equilibrium model in an uncertain environment	20
1.1. A Walrasian equilibrium model	20
1.2. Extension of the model	21
1.3. The linear case	23
2. Dynamic properties of the current expectation model	25
2.1. The rational expectations model	25
2.2. Comparison of the constrained and unconstrained reduced forms	27
2.3. Comparison of various expectation schemes	28
3. Learning processes	34
References	36
3. A Model with Future Expectations	37
1. Examples	37
1.1. Hyperinflation models	37
1.2. The Taylor model	39

	1.3. Some remarks on the price equation	40
	1.4. The evolution of an asset price	43
2.	A description of the solution methods	44
	2.1. The "forward" — "backward" approach	44
	2.2. Linear solutions	48
	2.3. The general solution	54
3.	Properties of the solution set	57
	3.1. Impact of a terminal condition	57
	3.2. Impact of an initial condition	57
	3.3. Sunspots	59
	3.4. Stationary solutions	60
	3.5. Variability of the linear stationary solutions	61
4.	Learning processes	63
References		66

4. Dynamic Extensions — 68

1.	Some examples	68
	1.1. A model with various expectations of the current endogenous variable	68
	1.2. A model with a two-periods-ahead future expectation	70
	1.3. A model with one current expectation and one future expectation	71
	1.4. Some remarks	72
2.	Solutions to the general univariate model	73
	2.1. The model	73
	2.2. Expression of the expectations in terms of realizations	74
	2.3. Constraints on the updating terms	75
	2.4. Some consequences	76
	2.5. Some applications	77
3.	Linear solutions	79
	3.1. The general form of the linear solutions	79
	3.2. (Asymptotic) stationarity of the linear solutions	79
	3.3. An example	81
References		82

5. Multivariate Models — 82

1.	Dynamic macroeconometric models	82
2.	A simple case	85
	2.1. The case without recursivities	86
	2.2. The special case of a nilpotent structural matrix	86

2.3. The general case	87
3. The general model	89
3.1. Canonical forms	89
3.2. Reduction of the canonical form	92
3.3. Reduction of the general model	94
3.4. Linear stationary solutions	97
4. Rational expectations and non-stationary models	98
4.1. Decomposition of an ARIMA series and cointegration	99
4.2. Application to rational expectations models	102
5. Concluding remarks	108
References	109

6. A Mean-Variance Model — 110

1. The model	110
1.1. Demand function of the speculators	110
1.2. Excess supply function of storable good	112
1.3. Equilibrium condition	112
2. Evolution of the equilibrium price	113
3. Risk premia	114
3.1. Asymptotic behavior of the solutions	114
3.2. Comparative statics	117
References	119

Index — 120

Introduction to the Series

Drawing on a personal network, an economist can still relatively easily stay well informed in the narrow field in which he works, but to keep up with the development of economics as a whole is a much more formidable challenge. Economists are confronted with difficulties associated with the rapid development of their discipline. There is a risk of "balkanization" in economics, which may not be favorable to its development.

Fundamentals of Pure and Applied Economics has been created to meet this problem. The discipline of economics has been subdivided into sections (listed at the back of this volume). These sections comprise short books, each surveying the state of the art in a given area.

Each book starts with the basic elements and goes as far as the most advanced results. Each should be useful to professors needing material for lectures, to graduate students looking for a global view of a particular subject, to professional economists wishing to keep up with the development of their science, and to researchers seeking convenient information on questions that incidentally appear in their work.

Each book is thus a presentation of the state of the art in a particular field rather than a step-by-step analysis of the development of the literature. Each is a high-level presentation but is accessible to anyone with a solid background in economics, whether engaged in business, government, international organizations, teaching, or research in related fields.

Three aspects of *Fundamentals of Pure and Applied Economics* should be emphasized:

— First, the object covers the whole field of economics, not only theoretical or mathematical economics.
— Second, the project is open-ended and the number of books is not predetermined. If new and interesting areas appear, they will generate additional books.

— Last, all the books making up each section will later be grouped to constitute one or several volumes of an Encyclopedia of Economics.

The editors of the sections are outstanding economists who have selected as authors for the series some of the finest specialists in the world.

J. Lesourne   *H. Sonnenschein*

Reduced Forms Of Rational Expectations Models*

LAURENCE BROZE
Université de Lille III, France and CORE, Belgium

CHRISTIAN GOURIÉROUX
CEPREMAP, Paris, France

ARIANE SZAFARZ
Centre d'Economie Mathématique et d'Econométrie de l'Université Libre de Bruxelles, Belgium

INTRODUCTION

The taking into account of expectations remains an important subject in macroeconomic model building. This monograph presents the most recent results concerning the formulation of models including rational expectations. In clarifying the technical aspects of these results, we hope to allow the reader — who is not necessarily familiar with the econometric literature treating models with rational expectations — to measure the impact of the rationality hypothesis formulated by Muth in 1961 and its repercussions, especially in terms of macroeconomic models.

Macroeconomic model building is habitually based on two major simplifications. On the one hand, macroeconomic models are constructed with reference to behavioral models under the hypothesis of existence of representative agents. No direct reference is made to individual behavior or to the heterogeneity of this behavior. Consequently a problem of aggregation arises, i.e. a problem concerning the microeconomic foundations of the model's equations. On

---

* We are grateful to two anonymous referees for their helpful comments. We thank J. Ablett for help in translation and Th. Mallé for typing this monograph. Our work received support from CEPREMAP, the Commissariat Général du Plan and from CEME and DULBEA (University of Brussels).

the other hand, the models are established using long term relations, these being essentially static equations.

These two major simplifications have been the object of an abundant literature, the broad outlines of which we will now mention. Regarding the problem of aggregation of individual behavior, it appears that models which are linear in their variables are relatively more robust than nonlinear models. We can thus accord a preference to this type of specification, quite apart from the fact that linear models afford simplicity. Consequently, in this monograph we will concentrate essentially on the study of linear models.

With regard to dynamics, this is introduced naturally at the macro level in the description of various phenomena. We can classify these phenomena into three categories, each of which merits a specific treatment. For example, one can distinguish:

a) dynamic processes of accumulation, of the "tendency" type, which aim to describe aspects of growth.

b) dynamic adjustment processes, which explain how long term equilibria are attained.

c) dynamic processes of anticipation, which take into account the effects of previsions formed by agents.

The introduction of dynamic components in macro models can be achieved in a variety of ways. One often proceeds by including some "dynamic" elements in a static model. Carried out in two stages, this procedure involves firstly establishing a static model expressing the long term relationship considered, then adding some lagged variables. This procedure incorporates some dynamic effects in the model without really distinguishing the three categories mentioned above. Often characterized as "ad hockery", it is associated methodologically with models including error correction.

An alternative method, "general to specific", is based on a statistical analysis of the joint evolution of the various time series associated with the variables of the model. Subsequently, one isolates, making reference to this study, certain structural relationships. Although it represents a quite different approach, this type of procedure is compatible with the first procedure mentioned above. Moreover, it would be desirable to combine both approaches.

In this monograph we will be specifically interested in one of the causes of dynamics, namely the presence of expectations. On the other hand, we will not consider in detail the other two causes cited. We will suppose, when we study the various models, that these two effects are summarized either by lagged variables or by a particular dynamic property of the exogenous variables.

Expectations of economic variables are mostly non-observable, at least at the macro level. Even when one has data available (notably from opinion surveys) on the previsions made by various categories of economic agents, these observations are essentially disaggregated. Three approaches can then be envisaged. The first involves aggregating the observations, making use of weighted means calculated using the method usually employed for the purposes of short term prevision. The second possibility involves a search for a summary measure of individual expectations which is based on a direct aggregation of microeconomic models. However, this approach is often very complicated and can only be easily developed under restrictive hypotheses.

Finally, the most commonly utilized approach involves forgetting completely individual observations and writing a subsidiary model or expectation scheme describing the formation of aggregated expectations. In fact the necessity of such scheme exceeds even the problem of non-observability of expectations. The presence of expectations can have an indirect effect (this effect forms the basis of Lucas' critique (1976)). Hence, even in the ideal case where one has available observations of previsions which are usable at the macro level, the mode of formation can remain important for the calculation of multipliers or economic policy simulations.

Expectation schemes can be divided into two broad categories:

a) Exogenous schemes that fix the method of calculating previsions independently of the structure of the model. In this category, one finds in particular the adaptive scheme. The facility offered by this type of approach lies in the replacement of expectations by "proxies" established outside the model.

b) Endogenous schemes for which there is simultaneous determination of the expectations and the other endogenous variables of the model. Notably, this category includes rational expectations, but it is much broader. The simultaneous nature of these schemes evidently renders the model more complex. However, it permits the formulation of a response to the critique of Lucas concerning the taking into account of structural modifications.

The rational expectations hypothesis as formulated by Muth (1961) is stated as follows: "The rational expectations are the same as the predictions of the relevant economic theory". Rational previsions are obtained by utilizing available information and a knowledge of the model. The expectations therefore depend on the structural parameters, and this has repercussions on the multipliers of the model.

The dynamic properties of the models are crucially linked to the scheme retained for the previsions. Thus the choice of an endogenous scheme can lead to a reduced form quite different from that deduced from an exogenous scheme, owing to the indirect effects. From this point of view, the originality of the rational expectations hypothesis *vis-à-vis* the adaptive expectations hypothesis lies essentially in rendering the previsions endogenous.

Plan of the monograph

This monograph includes six sections. The first section reviews briefly certain generalities concerning expectation schemes. It introduces the formal definitions of adaptive and rational schemes. The latter is defined as an optimal method of calculating the prevision based on the information available. We then examine the principal properties of these two schemes. In particular, those characteristics of rational expectations which permit the formulation of direct tests are illustrated with the aid of a concrete example.

Economic models with rational expectations can be divided into two broad classes according to whether or not they include expectations of future endogenous variables. In fact, for univariate models, the presence of multiple solutions concern exclusively models with expectations of future variables. In order to introduce the problems of reduction gradually, we commence by presenting, in section 2, a model including expectations of current variables only. This model is an extension of a Walrasian equilibrium model. In studying this model, we compare different expectation schemes and point out the specific indirect effect due to the endogenous nature of the rational scheme. Finally we present a learning process. It will become apparent that, in certain cases, the rationality hypothesis can be represented as the limit of a suboptimal mechanism for revising previsions.

Section 3 considers a model, probably the most well known model of rational expectations, which includes expectations of future variables. In its synthetic form, this model corresponds to the hyperinflation model of Cagan, to the Taylor model, and to the model of price determination of an asset traded on the stock exchange. This model admits an infinity of solutions, as evidenced by the presence of an arbitrary term in its reduced form. We consider successively various aspects of this phenomenon, which is specific to models with rational expectations. Essentially, we show how and why one may be led to give preference to some of these solutions.

At the end of sections 2 and 3, one could be tempted to believe that all the problems of reduction associated with the presence of rational expectations have been covered. In section 4 we show that this is far from being the case. In fact, a certain number of dynamic complications (notably expectations associated with different horizons) can seriously complicate the reduction technique to such a degree that most of the methods previously developed become unusable. Without devoting too much attention to the general results, we illustrate various possibilities of models presenting such "complications".

Section 5 is devoted to the reduction of multivariate models with rational expectations. These models require a specific treatment as soon as the constraints imposed on the structural parameters introduce singular matrices. After having indicated the general solution and stationary solutions of these models, we give particular attention to the non-stationary trajectories. The methodology of the literature on cointegration permits one to show, in particular, that the effects of expectational errors are only short term.

In the formulation of the linear models, we have adopted a simplification whereby the entire conditional distribution of the future variables is summarized by its first moment, i.e. the conditional expectation. In certain situations, notably in the context of micro models where risk has to be taken into account, it is indispensable to retain more than one moment of the conditional distribution. Section 6 illustrates this type of approach by envisaging a mean-variance model with rational expectations. Nonlinearity evidently leads to new reduction problems. In particular, one observes that the phenomenon of multiplicity can affect the growth paths of the solutions. It follows that, contrary to what is obtained with linear models, the effect of expectational errors on the tendency can be significant.

References

Lucas, R. E. (1976): "Econometric policy evaluation: a critique", in *The Phillips Curve and Labor Markets*, Karl Brunner (ed.), supplement to the *Journal of Monetary Economics*, **1**, 19–46.

Muth, J. F. (1961): "Rational expectations and the theory of price movements", *Econometrica*, **29**, 315–335.

1. EXPECTATION SCHEMES

1. Expectations

1.1. Basic notions

The values taken by a variable of interest, denoted y, may be unknown. This occurs for instance when information is needed on future values of some economic characteristics or on variables that influence the behavior of agents. In such circumstances, one may look for proxies $\tilde{y}$ of y. These proxies are henceforth called *predictions* or *expectations*.

Expectations are generally determined by using the available information about some other variables summarized by the notation x. The prediction of y is then written as:

$$\tilde{y} = f(x),$$

where f denotes the computational mechanism that describes the transition from the observable variables x to the expectation $\tilde{y}$ of y.

Thus, for a given *information set* $I = \{x\}$, the ways to derive expectations are as numerous as the possible choices of the mapping f. This mapping is often called the *expectation scheme*. In this presentation, we always consider the case where the approximated variable y and the variables x used to form the expectation are random variables. On the other hand, the computational mechanism f is assumed to be deterministic. Consequently, the expectation $\tilde{y}$ is stochastic since it is a deterministic mapping of random variables.

The *expectation problem* consists in the search for a well adapted prediction of y. It may be seen as the problem of choosing a stochastic proxy $\tilde{y}$ for the stochastic variable y. Generally, the proxy leads to some error, which is called the *prediction error*. The error is also stochastic: it is given by: $e = y - \tilde{y}$. A possible measure of the prediction error is provided by the mean square error defined by:

$$E\, e^2 = E(y - \tilde{y})^2, \tag{1.1}$$

where E denotes the expectation operator.

1.2. Successive predictions

We now consider predictions formed in successive time periods. For this purpose, it is necessary to introduce sequences of random variables that are indexed by time, called (time) *processes*. We will use the notation $y = (y_t, t \in \mathbf{Z})$ for the variables to be predicted and $x = (x_t, t \in \mathbf{Z})$ for those used to compute expectations.

Also, a sequence of information sets $I = (I_t, t \in \mathbf{Z})$ is required. The set denoted I_t represents the information available at time t. It is often formed from the observable variables by taking their past and current values:

$$I_t = \{x_t, x_{t-1}, x_{t-2}, \ldots\} = \{x_{t-j}, j \geq 0\}.$$

It follows that the available information grows with time (nothing is forgotten). At time $t+1$, the information set is obtained from the preceding one by adding the new observation x_{t+1}:

$$I_{t+1} = I_t \cup \{x_{t+1}\}.$$

In such a dynamic context, various prediction problems may be treated. Let us first consider a given date t and the information set I_t available at that time. It may be used to forecast various values of the process of interest y. These values may be written as y_{t+h}, $h \in \mathbf{Z}$, where h denotes the duration between time t (at which the prediction is formed) and time $t+h$ (at which y_{t+h} is realized). We call h the expectation *horizon*. Finally, the prediction of y_{t+h} formed at time t is represented by one of the following expressions:

$$_t\tilde{y}_{t+h} = f_{t,h}(x_t, x_{t-1}, \ldots) = f_{t,h}(I_t).$$

One thus obtains a twice indexed sequence of expectations. For a fixed value of t, variations of h result in a sequence of expectations of y_{t+h} made at the same date t. In turn, for a fixed value of $t+h=T$, variations of t produce a sequence of successive expectations of the same variable $y_T = y_{t+h}$ formed at various dates.

It is then possible to analyze the evolution of the expectations with respect to the increasing information sequence I. In particular, it is interesting to study the impact of an increase in the information occurring between two successive periods. This is given by:

$$_t\tilde{y}_T - {}_{t-1}\tilde{y}_T = f_{t,T-t}(I_t) - f_{t-1,f_{t-1,T-t+1}}(I_{t-1}).$$

This difference is the *updating* of the expectation process.

In practice, we usually fix a maximal horizon H and in such a case, the various predictions may be summarized by Table I, which is given for H = 3.

TABLE I

Date of the prediction	Variable to be predicted						
	y_T	y_{T+1}	y_{T+2}	y_{T+3}	y_{T+4}	y_{T+5}	y_{T+6}
T	y_T	$_T\tilde{y}_{T+1}$	$_T\tilde{y}_{T+2}$	$_T\tilde{y}_{T+3}$			
T+1	y_T	y_{T+1}	$_{T+1}\tilde{y}_{T+2}$	$_{T+1}\tilde{y}_{T+3}$	$_{T+1}\tilde{y}_{T+4}$		
T+2	y_T	y_{T+1}	y_{T+2}	$_{T+2}\tilde{y}_{T+3}$	$_{T+2}\tilde{y}_{T+4}$	$_{T+2}\tilde{y}_{T+5}$	
...	...	...	...	...	...	...	...

In this table, the sequence of expectations made at the same date is described by a given row and the updating of expectations is obtained with reference to a column.

2. Adaptive scheme

2.1. *The adaptive form*

The adaptive expectation scheme is one of the most frequent schemes used in macroeconometrics. It is due to Fisher (1930) [See also Arrow (1959), Nerlove (1958), Friedman (1957) for some "historical" applications of this scheme]. The basic idea is to define the expectation scheme using a simple updating formula. In this subsection, we only consider one-period-ahead predictions.

The expectation of y_{t+1} made at time t is taken as a convex combination of the last expectation, i.e. of y_t made at time $t - 1$, and the last available observation on the y process, y_t. Thus, one obtains the following expression:

$$_t\tilde{y}_{t+1} = \lambda \, _{t-1}\tilde{y}_t + (1 - \lambda) y_t, \qquad (1.2)$$

where the *smoothing coefficient* λ takes a value between 0 and 1.

Implicitly, the information used is assumed to be fully summarized by the values of $_{t-1}\tilde{y}_t$ and y_t. Subsequently, it will become apparent that this information set might also be viewed as composed of y_t, y_{t-1}, y_{t-2} ...

Furthermore the computational mechanism that leads from $_{t-1}\tilde{y}_t$ and y_t to $_t\tilde{y}_{t+1}$ involves a linear mapping with time-invariant coefficients λ and $1-\lambda$. It follows that the same formula is used at any time. In addition, linearity implies that adaptive expectations do not depend on the units used in the specification of the variable of interest y.

Equation (1.2) may be interpreted directly as an updating formula. Indeed, it is equivalent to:

$$_t\tilde{y}_{t+1} - {}_{t-1}\tilde{y}_t = (1-\lambda)(y_t - {}_{t-1}\tilde{y}_t). \tag{1.3}$$

The updating value depends linearly on the last observed prediction error. Since the smoothing coefficient λ is smaller than 1, a positive (negative) prediction error leads to an increase (a decrease) in the next expectation. Moreover, since λ is positive, the modification made to the last prediction is always smaller than the last error. Therefore, the *error correction* procedure appears to be generally partial.

On the other hand, the prediction mechanism obviously depends on the value chosen for the smoothing coefficient. A smaller value for λ gives a larger weight to the current observation. In the limiting case where the smoothing coefficient vanishes, the expectation coincides with the current observation and the expectation scheme is equivalent to the *naive* one:

$$_t\tilde{y}_{t+1} = y_t.$$

Finally, one can easily determine the evolutions of y so that adaptive expectations correspond to *perfect foresight* (i.e. no prediction error). By imposing:

$$_t\tilde{y}_{t+1} = y_{t+1}, \forall t,$$

one obtains from (1.3) the following recursive formula:

$$y_{t+1} - y_t = (1-\lambda)(y_t - y_t) = 0.$$

Thus, adaptive expectations are perfect when y is a constant process.

In all other cases, prediction errors occur. For instance, let us consider a process y exhibiting exponential growth:

$$y_t = A \rho^t,$$

where A and ρ are positive coefficients (they could be either deterministic or stochastic), with $\rho > 1$. The adaptive expectations are solutions of the following linear recursive equation:

$$_t\tilde{y}_{t+1} = \lambda\,_{t-1}\tilde{y}_t + (1-\lambda)A\rho^t.$$

The solutions may be written as:

$$_t\tilde{y}_{t+1} = \frac{(1-\lambda)A\rho^{t+1}}{\rho-\lambda} + C\lambda^{t+1},$$

where C is a real number.

If λ is strictly smaller than 1, then one has approximately for large values of t:

$$_t\tilde{y}_{t+1} \# \frac{1-\lambda}{\rho-\lambda} A\rho^{t+1}.$$

The prediction error becomes:

$$y_{t+1} - {_t\tilde{y}_{t+1}} \# \frac{1-\lambda}{\rho-\lambda} A\rho^{t+1} - A\rho^{t+1} = \frac{1-\rho}{\rho-\lambda} A\rho^{t+1}.$$

The prediction error is always negative. This example illustrates the partial correction mechanism of the adaptive scheme. Indeed, the expectation scheme is not flexible enough to capture the evolution of the variable. The absolute error becomes more and more important while the relative error remains constant (see Figure 1).

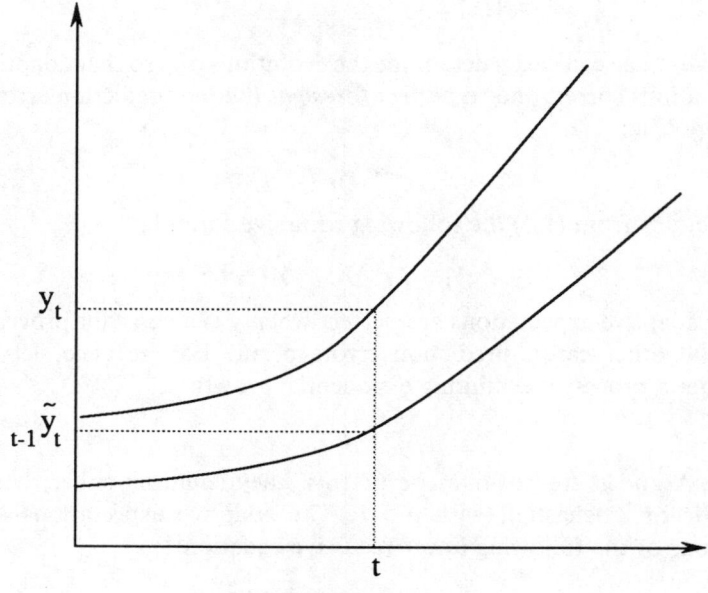

FIGURE 1

2.2. The extrapolative form

The updating formula that has been introduced does not define unambiguously the expectations. It has to be completed by an initial condition, i.e. by a given value of the expectation at an initial date.

In practice, the initial period is often taken as $t_0 = -\infty$ and the initial condition is stated as:

$$\lim_{t \to \infty} \lambda^{-t}{}_{t-1}\tilde{y}_t = 0.$$

Under this constraint, successive substitutions yield:

$$\begin{aligned}
{}_t\tilde{y}_{t+1} &= \lambda\,{}_{t-1}\tilde{y}_t + (1-\lambda)y_t \\
&= \lambda^2\,{}_{t-2}\tilde{y}_{t-1} + \lambda(1-\lambda)y_{t-1} + (1-\lambda)y_t \\
&= \lambda^j\,{}_{t-j}\tilde{y}_{t-j-1} + \sum_{k=0}^{j-1}(1-\lambda)\lambda^k y_{t-k} \\
&\vdots \\
&= \sum_{k=0}^{\infty}(1-\lambda)\lambda^k y_{t-k}.
\end{aligned}$$

A solution can only exist if the infinite sum, having $\lambda^k y_{t-k}$ as its general term, converges. It is then given by:

$$\begin{aligned}
{}_t\tilde{y}_{t+1} = (1-\lambda)y_t + (1-\lambda)\lambda y_{t-1} + \ldots \\
+ (1-\lambda)\lambda^k y_{t-k} + \ldots
\end{aligned} \quad (1.4)$$

Consequently, the prediction of y_{t+1} is seen to be based on the information represented by the current and past values of the process of interest. The weights affected to each component decrease exponentially. Further past values have less importance in the computation of the expectation. The special form of the weighting coefficients shows why this expectation scheme is also called *exponential smoothing*.

3. Rational scheme

3.1. Optimal predictions

Various criteria may be used in order to select an expectation scheme. Such criteria are, for instance, tractability, faithful reflections of the cycles existing in the evolution of y, or overall precision of the approximation procedure.

Since this precision is measured by the mean square error $E(y-\tilde{y})^2$, it seems quite natural to minimize this value. The minimization problem is then specified with respect to a given information set. Its formulation involves the choice of an expectation scheme among the set of mappings f describing the computational mechanisms (see Section 1.1). The following property gives the solution to the minimization problem.

Property (1.5): Let y be the variable to be predicted and $I = \{x\}$ the information set. There exists a mapping f such that $E[y-f(x)]^2$ reaches its minimal value. This mapping is the expectation of y conditional on x.

The conditional expectation is denoted $E[y|x]$ or $E[y|I]$. It is the mean of the conditional distribution of y given x. We will use the following terms interchangeably: *conditional expectation* (of y given x), *optimal prediction* (of y based on x), *rational expectation* (of y based on x).

3.2. Some properties of optimal predictions

The optimal prediction $E[y|x]$ may be seen as the orthogonal projection of y on the set of all mappings of x which are square-integrable, with the inner-product $\langle x, y \rangle = E(xy)$. This interpretation implies some important properties of the rational expectation scheme.

Property (1.6): The prediction error is orthogonal to the prediction:
$E\{(y - E[y|I]) E[y|I]\} = 0$.

Property (1.6) is a direct consequence of the optimality of the rational scheme. If it were not satisfied, i.e. if the prediction error was correlated with the information set, it could be possible to take into account this correlation and improve expectations.

If joint observations of realizations y_t and expectations $_{t-1}\tilde{y}_t$ are available, then one can compute the empirical counterpart $\frac{1}{T}\sum_{t=1}^{T}(y_t - {}_{t-1}\tilde{y}_t)_{t-1}\tilde{y}_t$ and examine whether it is close to zero. If it is not, then the hypothesis of rational expectations should be rejected. Such series of expectations and realizations may be obtained by a sample survey. In many European countries, economic agents (firms, households, financial institutions, . . .) are questioned at regular intervals on their expectations about the evolution of various economic variables. These data are collected in order to analyse the economic cycle. However, they may also be used to study the expectational behavior of economic agents. Table II gives the households' expectations and the realizations of the retail price index in France. These data are collected three times a year and regularly published in *Tendances de la Conjoncture* (INSEE).

TABLE II

Year	1980				1981				
True value	59.5	59.5	55.5	57.0	51.5	58.5	47.0	42.0	−3.0
Expectation	−10.0	4.5	−1.5	−4.0	−11.5	−19.5	−25.5	−13.5	15.0

Year	1983				1984			1985	
True value	1.5	25.0	20.5	20.0	20.0	21.0	12.0	2.0	−22.0
Expectation	−18.0	−9.0	−18.0	−15.5	−14.0	−14.5	−22.0	−23.5	−32.5

Year	1986			1987			1988
True value	−39.5	−48.0	−45.0	−42.0	−38.5	−44.0	−51.5
Expectation	−35.5	−7.5	−26.0	−16.5	−30.0	−32.0	−39.0

Figure 2 shows that the values predicted by the agents are generally lower than the true levels of the variable. However, this picture exhibits no clear evidence concerning the rationality of the expectation scheme. To test the rational expectation hypothesis, it is preferable to consider the joint observations of realizations and prediction errors. Figure 3

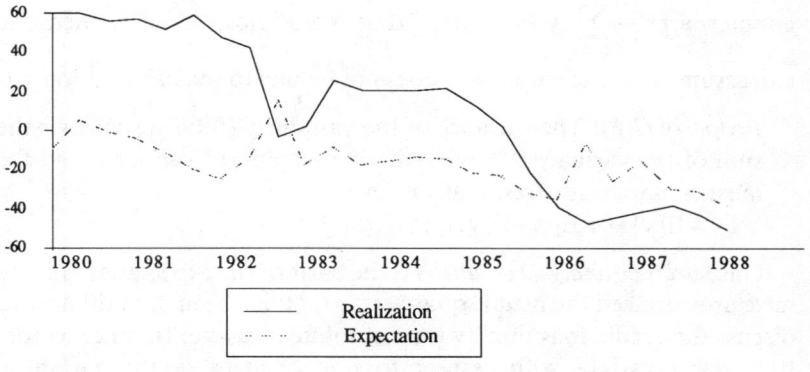

FIGURE 2

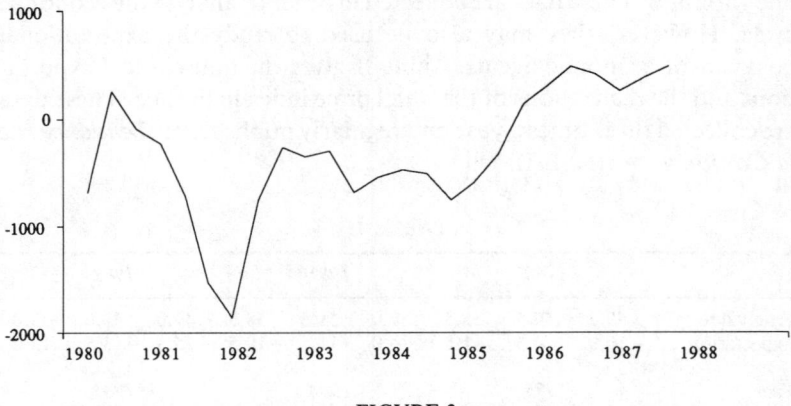

FIGURE 3

gives the series of products $(y_t - {}_{t-1}\tilde{y}_t)_{t-1}\tilde{y}_t$. Under the rational expectation hypothesis, this series should vary around zero. Clearly, this condition is not satisfied and rationality should probably be rejected for these particular variables.

Property (1.7): The prediction error is uncorrelated with any variable included in the information set:
$E\{(y - E[y|I])x_k\} = 0, \forall x_k \in I.$

If joint observations of realizations y_t, expectations ${}_{t-1}\tilde{y}_t$ and another variable x_{kt} are available, then one can compute the empirical counterpart $\frac{1}{T}\sum_{t=1}^{T}(y_t - {}_{t-1}\tilde{y}_t)x_{kt}$. If it is not close to zero, then one can assume that the variable x_k does not belong to the information set.

Property (1.8): The variance of the variable y (total variance) is the sum of the variance of the prediction (explained variance) and the mean square error (residual variance):
$Vy = VE[y|I] + E[y - E[y|I]]^2.$

This *variance analysis equation* is the basis of the expectation quality measures. Indeed the mean square error that has been used till now to discuss the predictions quality is an absolute measure. In other words, it is not invariant with respect to unit changes in the variables. Invariance is obtained with the relative measure defined by:

$$\frac{E[y - E[y|I]]^2}{Vy}.$$

As a consequence of the variance analysis equation, this measure takes values between 0 and 1. Furthermore, it is equal to 0 when the expectations are perfect, i.e. $y = E[y|I]$, and to 1 when the information set is the smallest one. In the latter case the rational expectation is given by the mean of the variable: $E[y|I] = Ey$.

Property (1.9) or Law of iterated predictions: Let I and J be two information sets such that J is included in I. The prediction of y based on J is equal to the prediction of $E[y|I]$ based on J: $E[E[y|I]|J] = E[y|J]$.

A consequence of property (1.7) or (1.9) is of great importance. Taking as a special case for J the smallest information set yields $E[y|J] = Ey$. It follows that *rational expectations are unbiased*:

$$E[E[y|I]] = Ey. \qquad (1.10)$$

The rational scheme does not allow for systematically positive or negative prediction errors. The property of unbiasedness may also be used for empirically testing rationality. From observations on realizations and expectations, it is possible to compute the empirical counterpart $\frac{1}{T}\sum_{t=1}^{T}(y_t - {}_{t-1}\tilde{y}_t)$. If this quantity is not close to zero, one would reject the hypothesis of rational expectations. Let us consider again the

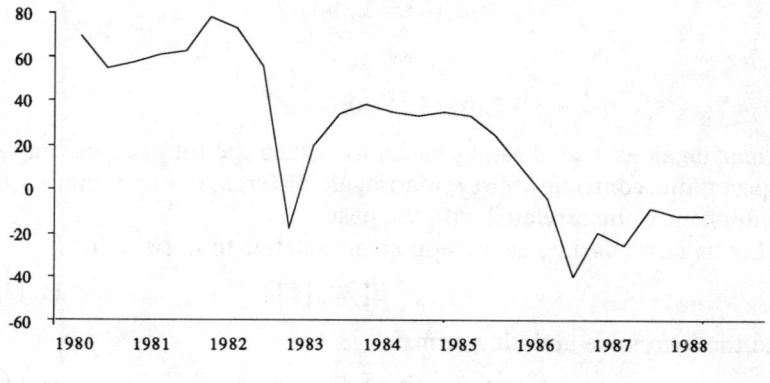

FIGURE 4

example of the French households' forecasts of the retail price. Figure 4 gives the prediction errors associated with these forecasts. Clearly, they don't fluctuate around zero and the rational expectation hypothesis should be rejected.

Property (1.11): The prediction error diminishes when the information set becomes larger:
$$I \supset J \Rightarrow E[y - E[y|I]]^2 \leq E[y - E[y|J]]^2.$$

The mean square prediction error is then linked to the quantity of available information.

3.3. Prediction errors and updating

We now consider a dynamic framework where $y = (y_t, t \in Z)$ is the process of interest and $I = (I_t, t \in Z)$ is the increasing sequence of information sets. At time t, I_t is given by $I_t = \{x_t, x_{t-1}, \ldots\}$. The preceding properties enable us to show some characteristics of the prediction errors and the updating. The notions of martingales and martingale differences will be needed, therefore we recall their definitions.

Definition (1.12): Let $I = (I_t, t \in Z)$ be an increasing sequence of information sets.

a) A process $M = (M_t, t \in Z)$ is a *martingale* if and only if
$$E[M_{t+1}|I_t] = M_t, \forall t \in Z.$$

b) A process $\Delta = (\Delta_t, t \in Z)$ is a *martingale difference* if and only if
$$E[\Delta_t|I_t] = \Delta_t, \forall t \in Z,$$

and
$$E[\Delta_{t+1}|I_t] = 0, \forall t \in Z.$$

A martingale is a stochastic process for which the rational and naive expectations coincide whilst a martingale difference is such that each component is uncorrelated with the past.

Let us now consider prediction errors relative to horizon h:

$$v_{t,h} = y_{t+h} - E[y_{t+h}|I_t], \tag{1.13}$$

and the successive updating terms:

$$\epsilon_t^h = E[y_{t+h}|I_t] - E[y_{t+h}|I_{t-1}]. \tag{1.14}$$

Following the law of iterated predictions on y, the updating term ϵ_t^h may also be written as:

$$\epsilon_t^h = E[y_{t+h}|I_t] - E[E[y_{t+h}|I_t]|I_{t-1}].$$

This may be interpreted as the one-period-ahead prediction error on the prediction of y_{t+h} made at time t. It follows from property (1.7) that the error ϵ_t^h is uncorrelated with all elements of the information set I_{t-1}: $E[\epsilon_t^h|I_{t-1}] = 0$.

Property (1.15): The sequence of updating terms (with horizon h), i.e. (ϵ_t^h, $t \in Z$), is a martingale difference for any fixed value of h.

On the other hand, the prediction errors are not martingale differences as soon as the horizon is larger than or equal to 2. They can however be expressed easily by means of such processes. Indeed, any prediction error may be written in terms of successive updating terms:

$$\begin{aligned} v_{t,h} &= y_{t+h} - E[y_{t+h}|I_t] \\ &= y_{t+h} - E[y_{t+h}|I_{t+h-1}] \\ &+ E[y_{t+h}|I_{t+h-1}] - E[y_{t+h}|I_{t+h-2}] \\ &\vdots \\ &+ E[y_{t+h}|I_{t+1}] - E[y_{t+h}|I_t], \end{aligned}$$

$$v_{t,h} = \sum_{i=0}^{h-i} \epsilon_{t+h-i}^i. \tag{1.16}$$

Other interesting results concern the evolution of the expectations of a given variable y_T. These expectations are given by:

$$_t\tilde{y}_T = E[y_T|I_t], \quad t \in Z.$$

As time goes on, these predictions are modified. The updating term from one period to another is:

$$\epsilon_t^{T-t} = E[y_T|I_t] - E[y_T|I_{t-1}], \quad t \in Z.$$

It has already been noted that updating terms are uncorrelated with the past. This implies the two following results:

Property (1.17): a) The updating sequence (ϵ_t^{T-t}, $t \in Z$) is a martingale difference.
b) The rational expectations sequence ($_t\tilde{y}_T = E[y_T|I_t]$, $t \in Z$) is a martingale.

An illustration of the second part of property (1.7) is provided by the sequence of forward prices on an efficient market. Indeed, if we let T denote the term of the contract, the forward price at time t < T is given by $E[p_T|I_t]$. It is the rational expectation of p_T formed using the available information I_t. It follows from property (1.17.b) that the forward prices sequence is a martingale (Samuelson (1965)).

Finally, it is possible to study the successive prediction errors. The prediction error, $v_{T-t,t} = y_T - E[y_T|I_t]$, is such that:

$$v_{T-t+1,t-1} = y_T - E[y_T|I_{t-1}]$$
$$= y_T - E[y_T|I_t] + E[y_T|I_t] - E[y_T|I_{t-1}]$$
$$= v_{T-t,t} + \epsilon_t^{T-t}.$$

It follows that the sequence $(v_{T-t,t}, t \in Z)$ is a martingale. This allows for a comparison between successive prediction errors.

Property (1.18): The mean square prediction error diminishes as t increases: $E(y_T - E[y_T|I_t])^2$ is a decreasing function of index t.

In practice, it is often assumed that the information set I_t includes the past and current values of the process y. In this case, for t larger than T,

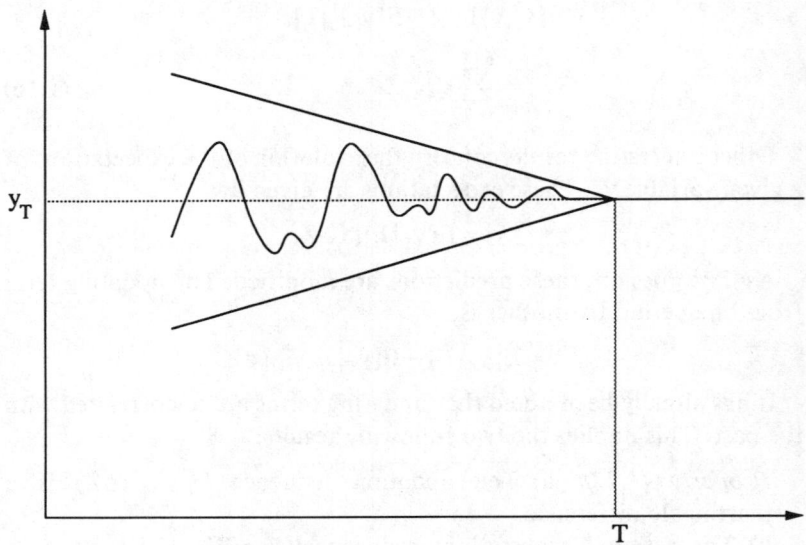

FIGURE 5

y_T belongs to the set I_t. It follows that y_T is known perfectly at time t: $E[y_T|I_t] = y_T$, $t \geq T$. The sequence of successive predictions of y_T together with the corresponding prediction intervals are illustrated in Figure 5. For instance, if y denotes the sequence of forward prices, Figure 5 shows that predictions become better as time draws nearer to the term.

References

Arrow, K. J. (1959): "Towards a theory of price adjustment", in Abramowitz, M. *et al.* (Eds), *The Allocation of Economic Resources*, Stanford University Press, 49-51.
Arrow, K. J. and Nerlove, M. (1958): "A note on expectations and stability", *Econometrica*, **26**, 297-305.
Brown, B. and S. Maital (1981): "What do economists know?: An empirical study of experts' expectations", *Econometrica*, **49**, 491-504.
Carlson, J. (1975): "Are price expectations normally distributed?", *Journal of the American Statistical Association*, **70**, 749-754.
Doob, J. (1953): *Stochastic Processes*, Wiley.
Fisher, I. (1930): *The Theory of Interest as Determined by Impatience to Spend Income and the Opportunity to Invest it*, New York, MacMillan.
Friedman, B. (1980): "Survey evidence and the rationality of interest rate expectations", *Journal of Monetary Economics*, **6**, 453-465.
Friedman, M. (1957): *A Theory of Consumption Function*, NBER, New York.
Gouriéroux, C. and J. Pradel (1985): "Direct test of the rational expectation hypothesis (with special attention to qualitative variables)", *European Economic Review*, **30**, 265-284.
Houthekker, H. (1961): "Systematic and random elements in short term price movements", *American Economic Review*, **51**, 164-172.
INSEE, *Tendances de la conjoncture*, n°4 March 1982, n°12 March 1984, n°20 March 1986, n°28 March 1988.
Kendall, M. (1964): "The analysis of economic time series, Part I: Prices", in Cootner, P. (Ed), *The Random Character of Stock Market Prices*, MIT Press, 85-99.
Lovell, M. (1986): "Test of the rational expectation hypothesis", *American Economic Review*, **76**, 110-124.
Mullineaux, D. (1978): "On testing for rationality: Another look at the Livingstone price expectations data", *Journal of Political Economy*, **86**, 329-336.
Nerlove, M. (1958): "Adaptive expectations and Cobweb phenomena", *Quarterly Journal of Economics*, **73**, 227-240.
Pesando, J. (1975): "A note on the rationality of the Livingstone price expectations", *Journal of Political Economy*, **83**, 849-858.
Samuelson, P. (1965): "Proof that properly anticipated price fluctuate randomly", *Industrial Management Review*, **6**, 41-49.
Turnowski, S. and M. Wachter (1972): "A test of the expectation hypothesis using directly observed wage and price expectations", *Review of Economics and Statistics*, **54**, 47-54.

2. A MODEL WITH CURRENT EXPECTATIONS

1. An equilibrium model in an uncertain environment

The model described in this section is concerned with price determination in a context where producers have to make decisions without knowing for sure the values of some variables influencing their economic environment. As a consequence, the equilibrium condition will include expectations of these variables. In order to emphasize the particularities of the model and discuss the underlying assumptions, we will briefly recall the classical Walrasian equilibrium model. As will be shown, this model corresponds to the perfect foresight case: it is based on the hypothesis of complete knowledge of the future.

1.1. A Walrasian equilibrium model

We consider the determination of the price in a market where two kinds of agents are involved: demanders and suppliers. Since we will mainly discuss the expectational behavior of the suppliers, a very simple formulation of the total demand function is retained.

Let p_t, q_t and z_{1t} denote respectively the price of the good at time t, the quantity demanded at time t and the vector of exogenous variables that influence the demand at time t. The inverse demand relation is given by:

$$p_t = D(q_t, z_{1t}), \qquad (2.1)$$

where $D(.,.)$ is a mapping that decreases with respect to its first argument (for a fixed value of the second argument).

Let us now consider the supply side of the model. All firms are assumed identical. Formally this yields a single firm problem. Let z_{2t} be the exogenous variables that influence the current production function. It follows that, for any quantity q, the cost function at time t is $C(q, z_{2t})$.

The firm's maximization problem is written as:

$$\underset{q_t}{\text{Max}}\ p_t q_t - C(q_t, z_{2t}).$$

Assuming a convex cost function, the solution to the maximization problem is deduced from the first order condition:

$$p_t = \frac{\partial C}{\partial q}(q_t, z_{2t}) \qquad (2.2)$$

Equation (2.2) shows that price and marginal cost are equal at the optimum. It can be rewritten with the use of the inverse marginal cost, denoted H $(., z_{2t})$, as:

$$q_t = H(p_t, z_{2t}). \qquad (2.3)$$

Finally, the equilibrium price p_t^e is obtained by equating the supply and demand quantities. It is thus the solution of the following equation:

$$p_t^e = D[H(p_t^e, z_{2t}), z_{1t}]. \qquad (2.4)$$

This price depends on the current period through the exogenous variables z_{1t} and z_{2t}. In other words, dynamics is present in Equation (2.4) but it is only caused by exogenous terms. No intrinsic endogenous dynamics appears.

1.2. Extension of the model

Let us now modify the preceding model and assume that the suppliers only know partially the price level p_t and the exogenous terms z_{1t} and z_{2t} at the time they make their decisions. There is thus a lag between the decision period and the realization of the variables.

Since profit is unknown, the suppliers are supposed to maximize their expected profit. Implicitly they are considered to be risk-neutral. More precisely, all variables appearing in the model are taken to be stochastic. The information available to the agents at time t is denoted I_{t-1}, hence the optimal prediction is given by $E[. | I_{t-1}]$. The new maximization problem based on optimal predictions is:

$$\underset{q_t}{\text{Max}} \ E[p_t q_t - C(q_t, z_{2t}) | I_{t-1}], \qquad (2.5)$$

where the optimization is carried out with reference to all quantities q_t that are expressed as functions of the available information I_{t-1}.

In this framework, the entrepreneur is *rational* in the sense that he/she knows the transition mechanism that leads from the information I_{t-1} to the forthcoming values p_t and z_{2t}. This transition is summarized by the conditional distribution of p_t and z_{2t} based on I_{t-1}. Let $d\pi[p_t, z_{2t} | I_{t-1}]$ denote this distribution. The expected profit may be written as:

$$\begin{aligned} E[p_t q_t - C(q_t, z_{2t}) | I_{t-1}] &= \int (p_t q_t - C(q_t, z_{2t})) \, d\pi[p_t, z_{2t} | I_{t-1}] \\ &= \{\int p_t d\pi[p_t, z_{2t} | I_{t-1}]\} q_t \\ &\quad - \int C(q_t, z_{2t}) \, d\pi[p_t, z_{2t} | I_{t-1}] \\ &= E[p_t | I_{t-1}] q_t - E[C(q_t, z_{2t}) | I_{t-1}]. \end{aligned}$$

In these derivations it has been supposed that q_t only depends on I_{t-1}. This is a consequence of the maximization formulation which requires q_t to be fixed at the time when only I_{t-1} is available.

The expected profit thus depends on both the expected price and expected costs. Note that the expectation of the cost function, i.e.:

$$C^a(q, I_{t-1}) = E[C(q, z_{2t})|I_{t-1}],$$

is, like the cost function itself, convex with respect to its first argument. Indeed:

$$C^a(\lambda_1 q_1 + (1-\lambda_1)q_2, I_{t-1}) = E[C(\lambda_1 q_1 + (1-\lambda_1)q_2, z_{2t})|I_{t-1}]$$
$$\leq E[\lambda_1 C(q_1, z_{2t}) + (1-\lambda_1) C(q_2, z_{2t})|I_{t-1}]$$
$$= \lambda_1 C^a(q_1, I_{t-1}) + (1-\lambda_1) C^a(q_2, I_{t-1}),$$

for $0 \leq \lambda_1 \leq 1$.

The first order condition giving the quantity supplied is:

$$E[p_t|I_{t-1}] = \frac{\partial C^a}{\partial q}(q_t, I_{t-1}).$$

We retain the preceding formulation of the demanders' behavior and denote by $H^a(., I_{t-1})$ the inverse of the expected marginal cost. It follows that the new equilibrium condition is:

$$p_t = D[H^a(E[p_t|I_{t-1}], I_{t-1}), z_{1t}]. \tag{2.6}$$

Equation (2.6) expresses the price in terms of price expectation, variables influencing the demand, and expectations of the exogenous influences on the supply (through the intermediary of the expected cost function). However, at this stage, the price remains implicitly given because it appears in both sides of (2.6). Nevertheless it can be made explicit in the following way:

a) Consider the expected inverse demand:

$$D^a(q, I_{t-1}) = \int D(q, z_{1t}) d\pi[z_{1t}|I_{t-1}].$$

A condition normally imposed on inverse demand function is that it must be decreasing with respect to quantity. This condition should also be satisfied by the expectation D^a.

b) On taking the optimal prediction of both sides of Equation (2.6) with respect to the information set I_{t-1}, one obtains:

REDUCED FORMS OF RATIONAL EXPECTATIONS MODELS

$$E[p_t | I_{t-1}] = D^a[H^a(E[p_t | I_{t-1}], I_{t-1}), I_{t-1}]. \quad (2.7)$$

The mapping $D^a[H^a(., I_{t-1}), I_{t-1}]$ is decreasing. Equation (2.7) generally admits a unique solution, i.e. it defines a unique path for the expectation process $E[p_t | I_{t-1}]$. Let $g^a(I_{t-1})$ denote this solution.

c) The equilibrium price in an uncertain environment is then obtained by replacing the expectation of Equation (2.6) by its expression:

$$p_t = D[H^a(g^a(I_{t-1}), I_{t-1}), z_{1t}]. \quad (2.8)$$

The current price depends on current values of the exogenous variables that influence the demand. It also depends on the expected values of all exogenous variables through H^a and g^a.

1.3. The linear case

The model presented in the preceding subsection is often considered in the particular case of a linear demand function and a quadratic cost function. Under these restrictions, one has:

$$\begin{cases} D(q, z_1) = \alpha(z_1)q + \beta(z_1), & \alpha(z_1) < 0, \\ C(q, z_2) = \tfrac{1}{2}\gamma(z_2)q^2 + \delta(z_2)q + \epsilon(z_2), & \gamma(z_2) > 0. \end{cases}$$

It follows that the expectations are:

$$\begin{cases} \dfrac{\partial C^a}{\partial q}(q, I_{t-1}) = E[\gamma(z_{2t}) | I_{t-1}]q + E[\delta(z_{2t}) | I_{t-1}], \\ H^a(p, I_{t-1}) = \dfrac{1}{E[\gamma(z_{2t}) | I_{t-1}]} p - \dfrac{E[\delta(z_{2t}) | I_{t-1}]}{E[\gamma(z_{2t}) | I_{t-1}]}, \\ D^a(q, I_{t-1}) = E[\alpha(z_{1t}) | I_{t-1}]q + E[\beta(z_{1t}) | I_{t-1}]. \end{cases}$$

Note that these mappings are different from one period to another because they depend on the information set used to make predictions.

The equilibrium condition given by Equation (2.6) describes the evolution of prices with respect to the diverse expectations entering the model. In the linear case, it is written as:

$$p_t = \dfrac{\alpha(z_{1t})}{E[\gamma(z_{2t}) | I_{t-1}]} E[p_t | I_{t-1}] - \alpha(z_{1t}) \dfrac{E[\delta(z_{2t}) | I_{t-1}]}{E[\gamma(z_{2t}) | I_{t-1}]} + \beta(z_{1t}). \quad (2.9)$$

Taking the expectation of both sides yields:

$$E[p_t|I_{t-1}] = \left(1 - \frac{E[\alpha(z_{1t})|I_{t-1}]}{E[\gamma(z_{2t})|I_{t-1}]}\right)^{-1}$$
$$\left(-E[\alpha(z_{1t})|I_{t-1}]\frac{E[\delta(z_{2t})|I_{t-1}]}{E[\gamma(z_{2t})|I_{t-1}]} + E[\beta(z_{1t})|I_{t-1}]\right)$$
$$= g^a(I_{t-1}).$$

Substituting for $E[p_t|I_{t-1}]$ in Equation (2.9) leads to an expression of the price in terms of the exogenous variables and their expectations:

$$p_t = \frac{\alpha(z_{1t})}{E[\gamma(z_{2t})|I_{t-1}]}\left(1 - \frac{E[\alpha(z_{1t})|I_{t-1}]}{E[\gamma(z_{2t})|I_{t-1}]}\right)^{-1}$$
$$\left(-E[\alpha(z_{1t})|I_{t-1}]\frac{E[\delta(z_{2t})|I_{t-1}]}{E[\gamma(z_{2t})|I_{t-1}]} + E[\beta(z_{1t})|I_{t-1}]\right)$$
$$- \alpha(z_{1t})\frac{E[\delta(z_{2t})|I_{t-1}]}{E[\gamma(z_{2t})|I_{t-1}]} + \beta(z_{1t}). \qquad (2.10)$$

In order to further simplify this expression, one may impose linearity with respect to the exogenous variables on the equation giving the price. For this purpose, one has to assume:

$$D(q, z_1) = \alpha q + z_1 \beta,$$
$$\frac{\partial C}{\partial q}(q, z_2) = \gamma q + \delta,$$

Equation (2.9) then has the form of a linear model. The explanatory variables are the expectations of the price and the exogenous variables entering the demand side:

$$p_t = \frac{\alpha}{\gamma} E[p_t|I_{t-1}] - \frac{\delta\alpha}{\gamma} + z_{1t}\beta. \qquad (2.11)$$

A model of this very simplified type was used by Muth (1961) in his seminal paper on rational expectations. Clearly this model is based on some very restrictive assumptions: risk neutrality of the suppliers, agents' knowledge of the transition from the information I_{t-1} to the curent price p_t, time-invariance of the supply function, linearity of the demand and supply functions, and constant marginal propensity to demand with respect to price. All of these assumptions might of course be questioned. However the next subsection will deal exclusively with simple models like (2.11). The aim is to emphasize their dynamic

REDUCED FORMS OF RATIONAL EXPECTATIONS MODELS

properties and to discuss the robustness of the dynamics with respect to the chosen expectation scheme.

2. Dynamic properties of the current expectation model

2.1. The rational expectations model

Before removing the expectation, the reduced form of the model is the following:

$$y_t = a\, E[y_t | I_{t-1}] + x_t\, b, \qquad (2.12)$$

where y and x denote, respectively, the endogenous variable (i.e. the price in the preceding model) and the exogenous variables (including the constant term). As before, "exogenous variables" means that the x variables are considered as fixed during the adjustment process towards the equilibrium at time t. Coefficients a and b are the reduced form parameters. They generally depend (in a non-linear way) on the structural parameters. As seen before, the last equation yields:

$$E[y_t | I_{t-1}] = E[x_t | I_{t-1}]\, \frac{b}{1-a}. \qquad (2.13)$$

It follows that:

$$y_t = E[x_t | I_{t-1}]\, \frac{ab}{1-a} + x_t\, b. \qquad (2.14)$$

Equation (2.14) shows that the dynamics of the endogenous process relies crucially on the evolution of exogenous processes and, more specifically, on the way current exogenous variables depend on the past information. It is thus necessary to complete the model by specifying:

a) the available information set I_{t-1};

b) the evolution of the exogenous processes (or only of their expectations).

To each specification corresponds a generally distinct dynamics of the endogenous process.

The perfect foresight case Firstly, assume that the available information set I_{t-1} includes the current values of the exogenous variables x_t. Whatever the evolution of the exogenous process, expectations are made without error: $E[x_t|I_{t-1}] = x_t$. The relation giving the current value of the endogenous variable, i.e. equation (2.14), becomes:

$$y_t = x_t \frac{ab}{1-a} + x_t b = x_t \frac{b}{1-a}.$$

It corresponds to the perfect foresight model

$$y_t = a y_t + x_t b.$$

As one could expect, the perfect foresight hypothesis appears as a special case of rational expectations associated with a sufficiently large information set. In other words, for the current expectations model, the perfect knowledge of current exogenous variables implies a perfect expectation of the current endogenous variable.

Partial ignorance of the future The rational expectation model is nevertheless more interesting when future variables are partially unknown. Suppose that, among the K explanatory variables x_t, $\bar{K}$ are perfectly known at time $t-1$, while the $\tilde{K} = K - \bar{K}$ others are not. Without loss of generality, the first category of variables is taken as the first $\bar{K}$ components of the vector x and is denoted $\bar{x}$. Conformably, the $\tilde{K}$ remaining variables are considered to belong to the second category and are denoted $\tilde{x}$. It follows that:

$$y_t = E[\bar{x}_t|I_{t-1}] \frac{a\bar{b}}{1-a} + E[\tilde{x}_t|I_{t-1}] \frac{a\tilde{b}}{1-a} + \bar{x}_t \bar{b} + \tilde{x}_t \tilde{b},$$

$$y_t = \bar{x}_t \frac{\bar{b}}{1-a} + E[\tilde{x}_t|I_{t-1}] \frac{a\tilde{b}}{1-a} + \tilde{x}_t \tilde{b}.$$

The model has to be completed by a specification of the expectations of the exogenous $\tilde{x}_t$. We assume here a linear scheme with an autoregressive form of order one:

$$E[\tilde{x}_t|I_{t-1}] = H_0 + \bar{x}_t H_1 + \bar{x}_{t-1} H_2 + \tilde{x}_{t-1} H_3 + y_{t-1} H_4 \qquad (2.15)$$

where H_0, H_1, H_2, H_3 and H_4 are matrices having respective sizes of $1 \times \tilde{K}$, $\bar{K} \times \tilde{K}$, $\bar{K} \times \tilde{K}$, $\tilde{K} \times \tilde{K}$ and $1 \times \tilde{K}$. Under specification (2.15), one obtains a dynamic model describing simultaneously y and $\tilde{x}$:

$$y_t = \frac{aH_0\tilde{b}}{1-a} + \bar{x}_t \frac{\bar{b} + aH_1\tilde{b}}{1-a} + \tilde{x}_t \tilde{b} + \bar{x}_{t-1} \frac{aH_2\tilde{b}}{1-a}$$

$$+ \tilde{x}_{t-1} \frac{aH_3\tilde{b}}{1-a} + y_{t-1} \frac{aH_4\tilde{b}}{1-a}, \qquad (2.16)$$

$$\tilde{\tilde{x}}_t = H_0 + \tilde{x}_t H_1 + \tilde{x}_{t-1} H_2 + \tilde{\tilde{x}}_{t-1} H_3 + y_{t-1} H_4 + v_t,$$

with $E[v_t | I_{t-1}] = 0$.

This system is a joint autoregressive representation of $(y, \tilde{\tilde{x}})$ conditional on the predetermined variables $\tilde{x}$. Such an expression leads itself to a statistical treatment involving parameter estimation and tests of the restrictions imposed by the rational expectation hypothesis. The next subsection is devoted to a discussion of the latter.

2.2. Comparison of the constrained and unconstrained reduced forms

Model (2.16) may be directly compared to the unconstrained reduced form:

$$\left. \begin{array}{l} y_t = \pi_0 + \tilde{x}_t \pi_1 + \tilde{\tilde{x}}_t \pi_2 + \tilde{x}_{t-1} \pi_3 + \tilde{\tilde{x}}_{t-1} \pi_4 + y_{t-1} \pi_5, \\ \tilde{\tilde{x}}_t = H_0 + \tilde{x}_t H_1 + \tilde{x}_{t-1} H_2 + \tilde{\tilde{x}}_{t-1} H_3 + y_{t-1} H_4 + v_t. \end{array} \right\} \quad (2.17)$$

Under assumption (2.15) concerning the expectations of $\tilde{x}_t$, the existence of a rational expectations model explaining the formation of y_t depends on the expression of the reduced coefficients. More precisely, such a model is possible if and only if there exist real values, a, $\tilde{b}$ and $\tilde{\tilde{b}}$ satisfying the following relations:

$$\pi_0 = \frac{aH_0\tilde{\tilde{b}}}{1-a}, \quad \pi_1 = \frac{\tilde{b} + aH_1\tilde{\tilde{b}}}{1-a}, \quad \pi_2 = \tilde{\tilde{b}},$$

$$\pi_3 = \frac{aH_2\tilde{\tilde{b}}}{1-a}, \quad \pi_4 = \frac{aH_3\tilde{\tilde{b}}}{1-a}, \quad \pi_5 = \frac{aH_4\tilde{\tilde{b}}}{1-a}.$$

This set of relations gives the system of constraints. It can be written in a shorter way by defining $c = (1-a)/a$ and $d = \tilde{b}/(1-a)$. The condition for existence of a rational expectations model then becomes:

$$\begin{array}{l} \exists\ c, d, \tilde{\tilde{b}}: c\pi_0 = H_0\tilde{\tilde{b}}, \ c\pi_1 = d + H_1\tilde{\tilde{b}}, \\ \pi_2 = \tilde{\tilde{b}}, \ c\pi_3 = H_2\tilde{\tilde{b}}, \ c\pi_4 = H_3\tilde{\tilde{b}}, \ c\pi_5 = H_4\tilde{\tilde{b}}. \end{array} \quad (2.18)$$

The constraints are expressed in terms of both the unconstrained parameters π_0, π_1, π_2, π_3, π_4, π_5, H_0, H_1, H_2, H_3 and H_4 and the auxiliary parameters, c, d and $\tilde{\tilde{b}}$. The latter can be interpreted only under the null hypothesis of rational expectations.

Furthermore, the constraints are simultaneously linear with respect to both types of parameters. This particularly simple form allows for the development of a Wald test of the rational expectations hypothesis that only makes use of linear least squares estimation procedures. Such an approach has been introduced by Szroeter (1983), Gouriéroux and Monfort (1989) and Gouriéroux, Monfort and Renault (1988) for mixed hypotheses. The steps are the following:

a) Determine the OLS estimators $\hat{\pi}$ and $\hat{H}$ of the unconstrained reduced form parameters.

b) Estimate by OLS the regression model given by:

$$\begin{cases} 0 = -\hat{\pi}_0 c + \hat{H}_0 \tilde{\tilde{b}} & + u_1, \\ 0 = -\hat{\pi}_1 c + \hat{H}_1 \tilde{\tilde{b}} + d + u_2, \\ \hat{\pi}_2 = \phantom{-\hat{\pi}_3 c + \hat{H}_2} \tilde{\tilde{b}} & + u_3, \\ 0 = -\hat{\pi}_3 c + \hat{H}_2 \tilde{\tilde{b}} & + u_4, \\ 0 = -\hat{\pi}_4 c + \hat{H}_3 \tilde{\tilde{b}} & + u_5, \\ 0 = -\hat{\pi}_5 c + \hat{H}_4 \tilde{\tilde{b}} & + u_6. \end{cases}$$

This yields estimators of the auxiliary parameters c, d and $\tilde{\tilde{b}}$ that are consistent under the rational expectations hypothesis.

c) Compute the asymptotic variance-covariance matrix of the error terms $u_1, \ldots u_6$ of the regression. Re-estimate the regression model by taking into account the correlations among the errors, i.e. apply the quasi-generalized least squares method. It may be shown [See Gouriéroux, Monfort and Renault (1988)] that the second step estimators of c, d and $\tilde{\tilde{b}}$ have asymptotic optimality properties. Also, the Wald statistic of the rational expectation hypothesis is equal to the sum of the squared residuals corresponding to the last regression [Szroeter (1983)].

In other words, a natural way to examine whether a rational expectations specification holds consists in first using an unconstrained vector autoregressive representation (VAR) [See for instance Sims (1980)] and then examining the satisfaction of the constraints due to the rationality hypothesis. Technically, as far as a linear current expectations model is concerned, this approach only necessitates simple statistical methods of the linear least squares type.

2.3. Comparison of various expectation schemes

Model (2.12) is given by:

$$y_t = a\, E[y_t | I_{t-1}] + x_t b.$$

Its expression summarizes in a single formula two quite different ideas. The first one is the impact of expectations on real values which may be singled out as:

$$y_t = a\,_{t-1}\tilde{y}_t + x_t b,$$

where $_{t-1}\tilde{y}_t$ is the expectation of the endogenous variable y_t formed at time $t-1$. The second one is the rational expectations hypothesis, i.e. the optimality of the expectation scheme with respect to the available information. Formally:

$$_{t-1}\tilde{y}_t = E[y_t | I_{t-1}].$$

In this subsection we keep the first part of the model and modify the second part. A discussion of the consequences of such a modification on the evolution of the endogenous process will then be pursued. In order to facilitate the discussion, we restrict it to the case of a single explanatory exogenous variable x. Furthermore, the latter is assumed to admit an autoregressive representation:

$$x_t = \rho x_{t-1} + \epsilon_t,$$

where ρ is a real number with modulus strictly smaller than 1 and $\epsilon = (\epsilon_t)$ is an independent white noise with variance σ^2. In this representation ρx_{t-1} is equal to the expectation of x_t given I_{t-1}, which implicitly implies that y does not linearly Granger-cause x.

The rational expectation model   When the expectation is rational and based on the information set $I_{t-1} = \{x_{t-1}, y_{t-1}, x_{t-2}, y_{t-2}, \ldots\}$, one has:

$$_{t-1}\tilde{y}_t = E[y_t | I_{t-1}] = \frac{b}{1-a} E[x_t | I_{t-1}] = \frac{b}{1-a} \rho x_{t-1},$$

because the optimal prediction of x_t is ρx_{t-1}. It follows that:

$$y_t = a\,_{t-1}\tilde{y}_t + b\,x_t = \frac{ab\rho}{1-a} x_{t-1} + b\,x_t.$$

Let us now introduce the lag-operator L that, when applied to a current variable (x_t or y_t), gives the variable lagged one period (respectively x_{t-1} or y_{t-1}). The joint evolution of y_t and x_t may then be written as:

$$\begin{cases} y_t = \left(\dfrac{ab\rho L}{1-a} + b\right) x_t, \\ (1 - \rho L)x_t = \epsilon_t. \end{cases}$$

Subsequently, the endogenous process may be expressed in terms of the innovation ϵ of the exogenous process:

$$y_t = \left(\frac{ab\rho L}{1-a} + b\right)(1 - \rho L)^{-1}\epsilon_t. \qquad (2.19)$$

Equation (2.19) shows that y has an autoregressive-moving average representation ARMA (1, 1). This process is stationary for all real values of the structural parameters a and b (with a ≠ 1).

On the other hand, it is interesting to examine the effect of an exogenous shock on the endogenous variable. The usual way to do this is to define an exogenous shock by means of the innovation process [see Sims (1980)]. To a sustained shock $\Delta\epsilon$ to the components of the noise correspond the following modifications:

.on the exogenous x_t $\quad :\Delta x = \dfrac{1}{1-\rho}\Delta\epsilon;$

.on the expectation $_{t-1}\tilde{y}_t$ $\quad :\Delta\tilde{y} = \dfrac{b\rho}{(1-a)(1-\rho)}\Delta\epsilon;$

.on the endogenous y_t $\quad :\Delta y = \dfrac{1}{1-\rho}\left(\dfrac{ab\rho}{1-a} + b\right)\Delta\epsilon.$

Hence a modification of the evolution scheme of the exogenous process has a double effect on the endogenous process. The first effect is direct since it comes from the term bx_t. The second effect is indirect because it is transmitted through the expectation. Translated into a formula, this distinction is expressed by:

$$\frac{\Delta y}{\Delta \epsilon} = \underbrace{\frac{ab\rho}{1-a}\frac{1}{1-\rho}}_{\text{indirect effect}} + \underbrace{b\frac{1}{1-\rho}}_{\text{direct effect}},$$

or equivalently:

$$\frac{\Delta y}{\Delta x} = \underbrace{\frac{ab\rho}{1-a}}_{\text{indirect effect}} + \underbrace{b}_{\text{direct effect}}. \qquad (2.20)$$

Note that the size of the indirect effect depends on the parameter ρ describing the dynamics of the exogenous process.

The adaptive expectation model Another classical expectation scheme is the adaptive one. It was first introduced into a model by Fischer (1930) and its main properties have been systematically presented by Arrow (1959) and Nerlove (1958).

Following the adaptive scheme (see Section 1), the expectation $_{t-1}\tilde{y}_t$ is a weighted average of the last expectation and the most recent observation of the variable. Letting λ denote the weight:

$$_{t-1}\tilde{y}_t = \lambda\,_{t-2}\tilde{y}_{t-1} + (1-\lambda)y_{t-1}, \quad 0 \le \lambda \le 1,$$

or equivalently:

$$_{t-1}\tilde{y}_t - _{t-2}\tilde{y}_{t-1} = (1-\lambda)(y_{t-1} - _{t-2}\tilde{y}_{t-1}), \quad 0 \le \lambda \le 1.$$

The second form refers to the updating formula (2.3). Under the adaptive expectations hypothesis, the structural form of the model implies:

$$y_t - \lambda y_{t-1} = a(_{t-1}\tilde{y}_t - \lambda\,_{t-2}\tilde{y}_{t-1}) + (x_t - \lambda x_{t-1})b$$

Finally, we obtain:

$$(1 - (a+\lambda-a\lambda)L)y_t = b(1-\lambda L)x_t = \frac{b(1-\lambda L)}{1-\rho L}\epsilon_t$$

The last equation shows an autoregressive-moving average structure. However it does not always lead to a stationary solution y. The condition for stationarity requires the value of the parameter $\lambda + a(1-\lambda)$ to be strictly included in the real interval $(-1, 1)$. Equivalently, parameter a has to be such that $1 - 2/1 - \lambda < a < 1$. Figure 6 represents the admissible zone for stationarity. Larger values of the smoothing constant λ lead to larger intervals of admissible values for a.

When the stationarity condition is met, the effect of a sustained shock on the exogenous process is given by:

$$\frac{\Delta y}{\Delta x} = \frac{b(1-\lambda)}{1-(\lambda+a(1-\lambda))} = \frac{b}{1-a},$$

$$\frac{\Delta y}{\Delta x} = \underset{\text{indirect effect}}{\frac{ab}{1-a}} + \underset{\text{direct effect}}{b}. \qquad (2.21)$$

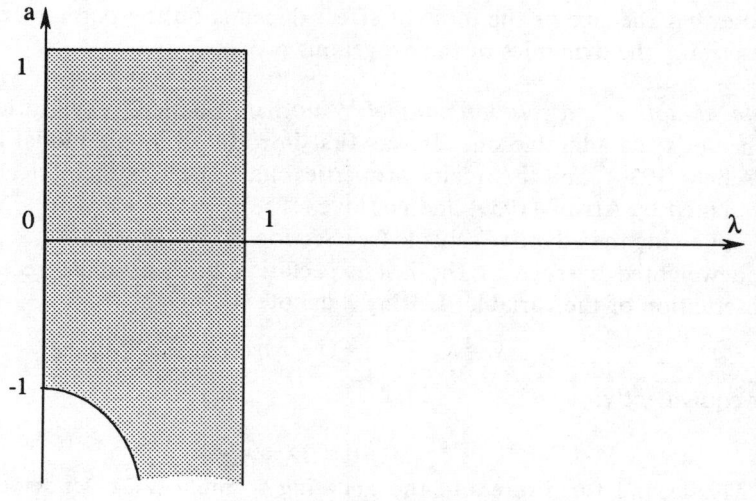

FIGURE 6

Here again appears a distinction between the direct effect of x and the indirect effect passing through the expectation. However, since the adaptive expectation has been chosen independently from the exogenous process, the indirect effect does not depend on ρ. Neither does it depend on the smoothing constant λ.

The limit case where both schemes are alike The adaptive scheme makes use of the information available at time $t-1$. Indeed the expectation may be written as:

$$_{t-1}\tilde{y}_t = \sum_{i=0}^{\infty} (1-\lambda)\lambda^i y_{t-i-1}.$$

It depends on all lagged endogenous variables. However it is generally not optimal. Optimality would be attained if the following relations occured simultaneously:

$$\begin{cases} _{t-1}\tilde{y}_t = (1-\lambda)y_{t-1} + \lambda\,_{t-2}\tilde{y}_{t-1} \\ _{t-1}\tilde{y}_t = E[y_t | I_{t-1}], \end{cases}$$

or equivalently if:

$$E[y_t | I_{t-1}] = (1-\lambda)y_{t-1} + \lambda E[y_{t+1} | I_{t-2}].$$

In the present context, the prediction error on y_t is proportional to ϵ_t:

$$y_t - E[y_t | I_{t-1}] = C\epsilon_t,$$

where the multiplicative factor C is in fact equal to the structural coefficient b. Thus the condition for optimality of the adaptive expectation may be reformulated, after replacing the conditional expectation, as:

$$y_t - C\epsilon_t = (1-\lambda)y_{t-1} + \lambda(y_{t-1} - C\epsilon_{t-1}),$$

or

$$y_t - y_{t-1} = C\epsilon_t - \lambda C\epsilon_{t-1}.$$

In words, the endogenous process should be such that the differentiated series is a stationary moving-average process of order 1.

Compare now the latter condition to the expression (equation (2.19)) of the rational expectation solution. It appears that the equivalence of adaptive and rational schemes is only possible in the limit cast $\rho = 1$, i.e. when the exogenous process is a random walk. Moreover, it is necessary that the smoothing constant satisfies:

$$\lambda = -\frac{a\rho}{1-a} = -\frac{a}{1-a}.$$

This result was established by Muth (1960). It emphasizes the fundamental difference between the rational and adaptive frameworks. In the adaptive case, the coefficient λ is generally chosen without referring to the dynamics of the exogenous process, while in the rational case — even when it has an adaptive interpretation — the expectation formation has to be linked to the structural parameters of the model (a, b and ρ in the present model). An important consequence of this distinction concerns economic policy. Suppose that the economic authority uses the process x as an instrument for influencing y. In our context, its choice will involve the fixation of a value for the correlation parameter ρ. Under rational expectations, variations in ρ affect the way agents predict future values of y [see Lucas (1976)]. Their expectation scheme is thus sensitive to changes in the exogenous dynamics. In turn, under adaptive expectations, whatever the value of ρ, expectations of future y's remain the same. The adaptive scheme does not capture changes in economic policy.

3. Learning processes

It is common postulated that the decisions of economic agents are based to a large degree on their views about future events. However, controversies arise as soon as the choice of an expectations model is considered. The rationale of the prediction mechanism of "real" agents is not yet fully elucidated (will it ever be?).

A comparison of diverse expectation schemes (rational, adaptive, perfect, etc.) may be carried out at a theoretical level and then confronted with empirical data. Unfortunately all test procedures generally treat jointly the structural relations, linking actual variables and expectations, and the expectation scheme. Another way to investigate the plausibility of a given expectation scheme will be outlined in this subsection. The basic idea is to examine whether there exists a theoretical explanation of the choice of the given scheme. More precisely, the rational expectation hypothesis implicitly includes the idea that agents know the transition probabilities from the past to the present. It thus naturally raises the problem of how agents can acquire such knowledge. Learning processes provide a possible answer to this problem.

The conditions for existence of a learning process are the following. Firstly, the relations among variables must hold with some degree of dynamic stability (especially if the variables are assumed stationary). Secondly, the agents must have enough time (theoretically an infinite period) to complete the learning process.

All learning models given in the literature (see e.g. Bray (1982), Bray and Savin (1986), Fourgeaud, Gouriéroux and Pradel (1986)) are based on the same principle. At time t, the agent makes use of a generally suboptimal expectation mechanism. This leads to a certain prediction that influences the realization of the endogenous variable. At time $t + 1$, the agent observes an additional endogenous variable that may be compared to the earlier prediction. On the basis of this comparison, the agent measures his/her expectation error and uses this information in order to modify the way he/she forms expectations.

In what follows, we describe a learning model along these lines. Furthermore, the deviation from one expectation modification to another is assumed to be very large (actually infinite) compared to the duration between the observations.

Let us return to the model presented in Subsection 2.3, i.e.:

REDUCED FORMS OF RATIONAL EXPECTATIONS MODELS

$$\begin{cases} y_t = a_{t-1}\tilde{y}_t + x_t b \\ x_t = \rho x_{t-1} + \epsilon_t, \end{cases}$$

and assume that the agent forms his/her expectation using the following formula:

$$_{t-1}\tilde{y}_t^{(1)} = C_1 x_{t-1},$$

where C_1 is a given real number. The realization of y_t is then such that:

$$y_t = a C_1 x_{t-1} + x_t b.$$

By observing during a sufficiently long period the relations occuring among y_t, x_{t-1} and x_t, the agent should perceive that the predictions of y_t is not $C_1 x_{t-1}$ but:

$$E[y_t | I_{t-1}] = a C_1 x_{t-1} + x_{t-1} \rho b.$$

The agent is thus spontaneously induced to modify his/her way of forming expectations. The earlier scheme will be replaced by:

$$_{t-1}\tilde{y}_t^{(2)} = C_2 x_{t-1},$$

where $C_2 = a C_1 + \rho b$. Again this new rule will be revealed erroneous and will be modified, and so on.

Let $_{t-1}\tilde{y}_t^{(k)} = C_k x_{t-1}$, denote the successive expectation formulations used by the learning agent. Iteration of the preceding argument yields:

$$C_k = a C_{k-1} + \rho b, \forall k.$$

The sequence of coefficients satisfies a recursive linear equation of order 1. A particular solution to this equation is given by $\overline{C} = b\rho/1 - a$. this is exactly equal to the coefficient associated with the rational expectation. The evolution of the sequence (C_k) is described by:

$$C_k = \frac{b\rho}{1-a} + \mu a^k, \quad \mu \in \mathbb{R}. \tag{2.22}$$

Two cases can be distinguished:

a) if $|a| < 1$, the sequence (C_k) converges to $\overline{C} = \frac{b\rho}{1-a}$.

Following the learning process, the agent is asymptotically rational;

b) if $|a| \geq 1$, the learning process does not converge and may not be used as a justification for the rational expectations hypothesis.

The learning process that has been described here is of course highly simplified. It could be made more sophisticated by introducing, for instance, continuous updatings, i.e. by allowing changes in the coefficients C_k at any point in time. Technically this leads to convergence conditions that are much harder to derive but which remain fundamentally of the same form. One might also think of introducing costs involved in information acquisition. Intuitively these costs would prevent convergence to rationality. Therefore learning could lead to rational expectations only in the limit case of zero costs.

References

Arrow, K. J. (1959): "Towards a theory of price adjustment", in *The Allocation of Economic Research Resources*, M. Abramowitz et al. (Eds), Stanford University Press, 49-51.

Bray, M. (1982): "Learning, estimation and the stability of rational expectations", *Journal of Economic Theory*, 26, 318-340.

Bray, M. and N. Savin (1986): "Rational expectations equilibria, learning and model specification", *Econometrica*, 54, 1129-1160.

Fisher, J. (1930): *The Theory of Interest as Determined by Impatience to Spend Income and the Opportunity to Invest it*, MacMillan, New York.

Fourgeaud, C., C. Gouriéroux and J. Pradel (1986): "Learning procedures and convergence to rationality", *Econometrica*, 54, 845-868.

Gouriéroux, C. and A. Monfort (1988): "A general framework for testing a null hypothesis in a mixed form", *Econometric Theory*, 5, 63-82.

Gouriéroux, C., A. Monfort and E. Renault (1988): "Tests d'hypothèses bilinéaires", *Essais en l'Honneur d'E. Malinvaud*, Economica, Paris.

Grossman, S. (1981): "An introduction to the theory of rational expectations under asymmetric information", *Review of Economic Studies*, 4, 103-124.

Lucas, R. E. (1976): "Econometric policy evaluation: a critique", in *The Phillips Curve and Labor Markets*, Karl Brunner (ed.), supplement to the *Journal of Monetary Economics*, 1, 19-46.

Muth, J. R. (1960): "Optimal properties of exponentially weighted forecasts", *Journal of the American Statistical Association*, 55, 229-305.

Muth, J. R. (1961): "Rational expectations and the theory of price movement", *Econometrica*, 24, 315-335.

Nerlove, M. (1958): "Adaptive expectations and Cobweb phenomena", *Quarterly Journal of Economics*, 73, 227-240.

Radner, R. (1983): "Comment on convergence to rational expectations equilibrium", in *Individual Forecasting and Aggregate Outcomes: "Rational Expectations" Examined*, R. Frydman and E. S. Phelps (eds), Cambridge University Press, Cambridge.

Sheffrin, S. (1983): *Rational Expectations*, Cambridge University Press, Cambridge.

Sims, C. A. (1980): "Marcoeconomics and reality", *Econometrica*, 48, 1551-1567.

Szroeter, J. (1983): "Generalized Wald methods for testing nonlinear implicit and overidentifying restrictions", *Econometrica*, 51, 335-353.

Wallis, K. (1980): "Econometric implications of the rational expectations hypothesis", *Econometrica*, 48, 49-73.

3. A MODEL WITH FUTURE EXPECTATIONS

1. Examples

The Muth model is a rational expectation model involving a current endogenous expected variable. More precisely, the structural form of the model consists of an equation explaining the endogenous variable y_t in terms of the expectation $E[y_t | I_{t-1}]$ and various exogenous variables among which some are observable and some are not. As shown in section 2, this equation has a unique solution. This uniqueness property greatly simplifies the analysis. It is also useful for practical purposes.

In this section we consider a modified version of the model. Formally, the change introduced in the original model might seem *a priori* rather small since it consists in replacing the current expectation $E[y_t | I_{t-1}]$ by the future expectation $E[y_{t+1} | I_t]$. However, as will be shown, this modification has a fundamental impact on the resolution of the model. Indeed a rational expectation model including future expectations admits multiple solutions. A detailed analysis of the whole set of solutions is thus required for this type of model.

1.1. Hyperinflation models

Models involving future rational expectations have been proposed in the literature to describe hyperinflation, i.e. large and rapid increase in the price level. These movements are normally accompanied by other economic phenomena, either linked to them or occuring simultaneously, such as a large supply of money.

The extreme situation of Hungary during the period August 1945–July 1946, described by Shiller (1978), illustrates this point. The nominal money supply was then multiplied by a factor of 10^{25} while the price level increased by a factor of 4×10^{27}. In this particular case, the inflation rate was larger than the rate of growth of the money supply. A possible explanation of this fact lies in the reduced liquidity preference of agents who wished to cover the expected loss of their purchasing power due to inflation.

To describe such complex phenomena, simultaneous equations models are needed. They must provide explanations of the main linkages existing between the relevant economic variables such as prices, the money supply and quantities produced, as well as the equilibrium formation on the different markets. The expectations generally concern the prices.

A first step in solving the model consists in specifying a partially reduced form equation which expresses the current price in terms of expected prices and exogenous factors. The solution to this equation provides the price path. It then becomes possible to determine the evolution of all the other variables, with reference to the price path obtained.

Hyperinflation models are generally constructed on the same basis as the usual macromodels, therefore they present the same advantages and disadvantages as these macromodels. So, they are often highly aggregated and thus do not explicitly refer to the behavior of individual agents. Also, these models only take into account a small number of variables and conceal some indirect effects that could be of great importance. Moreover, linearity with respect to all variables is one of the most common features. It is justified by practical needs, especially those presented by estimation and multiplicators analysis. From this point of view, effectiveness often dominates realism. In particular, when expectations are incorporated as explanatory variables, they are usually included in a linear way.

In a linear rational expectations model, the agents' views on future events are thus only captured by the first-order conditional moments. Consequently, such models reflect neither the influences of the variability that could arise among individual views, nor the potential effects of the expected variability. Indeed the inclusion of effects such as these would require the taking into account of second-order conditional moments.

The previous remarks are related to hyperinflation models as originally formulated by Cagan (1956) and developed under the rational expectations hypothesis by a large number of authors [e.g. Blanchard (1979), Sargent and Wallace (1973, 1975), Shiller (1978)]. However, they are not specific to this type of model, since they apply to any macromodel including expectations. In order to provide various illustrations of rational expectations models including future expectations, we will now give a formal presentation of Taylor's model and discuss its underlying assumptions in details. We will end the subsection with the presentation of an asset pricing model.

1.2. The Taylor model

We take here a slightly simplified version of the Taylor (1977) model. It is a stochastic macromodel describing the simultaneous equilibria in the aggregated goods (output) market and the money market. Price expectations are introduced by means of the demand function for goods. The two markets are linked through a real balance effect. The model has the following form:

$$\left.\begin{aligned} y_t &= -a_1[r_t - (_t\tilde{p}_{t+1} - p_t)] + a_2(m_t - p_t) + u_{1t}, \\ y_t &= b_0 + b_1(m_t - p_t) + u_{2t}, \\ m_t &= y_t + p_t - c_1 r_t + c_2(m_t - p_t) + u_{3t}, \\ m_t &= u_{4t}, \end{aligned}\right\} \quad (3.1)$$

where y_t, m_t, p_t and r_t denote respectively the log of the output, the log of the nominal money stock, the log of the price of goods and the nominal interest rate. $_t\tilde{p}_{t+1}$ is the expectation of the log of the future price, formed in the current period. The deviation $_t\tilde{p}_{t+1} - p_t$ appears as the expectation of $\log P_{t+1} - \log P_t$, where P represents the price of the goods. Furthermore, we have:

$$\log P_{t+1} - \log P_t = \log \frac{P_{t+1}}{P_t}$$
$$= \log\left(1 + \frac{P_{t+1} - P_t}{P_t}\right).$$

When $(P_{t+1} - P_t)/P_t$ is small, the previous expression may be approximated by $(P_{t+1} - P_t)/P_t$. This argument justifies the use of $_t\tilde{p}_{t+1} - p_t$ as a proxy for the expected inflation rate (between t and t + 1).

The model includes four endogenous variables y_t, m_t, p_t and r_t. The exogenous variables influencing the demand and the supply are summarized by the residual terms u_{1t}, u_{2t}, u_{3t}, u_{4t}.

The first equation represents the aggregate demand function. It depends negatively ($a_1 > 0$) on the expected real interest rate, i.e. the difference between the nominal interest rate and expected inflation, and positively on the real balances ($a_2 > 0$). This may be interpreted as a preference for holding goods when the real money balances are considered to be excessive. The second equation describes the supply of goods, which, in addition to the exogenous effects represented by u_{2t}, depends positively on real balances ($b_1 > 0$). The demand for money in

(3.1) has been formulated following a "Cambridge-type equation": $M_t = k P_t Y_t$ (where capitals denote the variables themselves, not their logs). The proportionality coefficient k, linking the demand for money to output, depends both on the interest rate and real balances. The money supply is assumed to be exogenous.

The structural form (3.1) may be easily transformed into a partially reduced form, such that each endogenous variable is expressed in terms of the expected future price and exogenous variables. One obtains a four-equation model giving respectively y_t, m_t, p_t and r_t in terms of $_t\tilde{p}_{t+1}$, u_{1t}, u_{2t}, u_{3t} and u_{4t}. The resolution may be performed recursively by analysing first the *price evolution equation* and secondly the consequences of the price evolution on the three other endogenous variables. In the model examined here, the price equation only involves the expected price and exogenous terms and may be solved without considering explicit forms of the other endogenous variables. On the other hand y_t, m_t and r_t can be determined only after having found the expression for the expected price.

From the structural form, we deduce the price evolution equation:

$$p_t = a\,_t\tilde{p}_{t+1} + u_t, \qquad (3.2)$$

where a is a reduced form parameter obtained from the structural parameters by the relation:

$$a = \frac{-a_1 c_1}{c_1 b_1 + a_1 c_2 - a_1 + a_1 b_1 - a_2 c_1},$$

and u_t is a linear combination of u_{1t}, u_{2t}, u_{3t} and u_{4t} with coefficients depending on the values taken by the structural parameters.

At this stage, the derivations have been made independently of any assumption about the expectation scheme. Let us now incorporate into the model the rational expectations hypothesis. Equation (3.2) becomes:

$$p_t = a\, E[p_{t+1} | I_t] + u_t, \qquad (3.3)$$

where I_t denotes the available information set at time t.

1.3. Some remarks on the price equation

Before going further and solving equation (3.3), we will examine more closely the initial structural form of our model. In fact, the following remarks are not specific to the Taylor model. They apply to a large class of models suggested in the literature which lead to a price evolution equation having a formal expression similar to (3.2) [see e.g. Cagan (1956), Lucas (1973), Sargent and Wallace (1973a, 1973b, 1975), Shiller (1978) . . .]. Furthermore, these remarks mainly concern the underlying structural form called the *ad hoc model* by Sargent and Wallace (1975), here (3.1), and not the expectation scheme (whether rational or not) chosen by the model builder.

a) Consider a hyperinflation model. It seems reasonable to postulate, at least as a first approximation, exponential evolutions for the price level and money supply:

$$P_t = P_0 g_0^t, \qquad M_t = M_0 g_1^t.$$

By taking logs, we obtain:

$$\begin{cases} p_t = \log P_0 + t \log g_0, \\ m_t = \log M_0 + t \log g_1. \end{cases}$$

Thus, as far as a hyperinflation model is concerned, solutions to the price (in log) equation should be sought among explosive (non-stationary) paths.

b) On the other hand, certain variables should not present an explosive behavior. For instance, consider the real interest rate $r_t - (_t\tilde{p}_{t+1} - p_t)$. This variable has a more appealing interpretation as an adjustment factor.

Now assume non-explosive exogenous variables and consider, for instance, the demand for goods. This demand includes "stationary" as well as "non stationary" terms. Such a formulation is feasible only if the explosive series, here m_t and p_t, have the same growth rate $g_0 = g_1$. This condition is obviously very strong and should be investigated empirically before concluding the formulation of any hyperinflation model.

c) Let us pursue the analysis further and consider the money supply equation. It seems realistic to impose the restriction that y_t and r_t are either stationary variables or explosive variables but with velocities smaller than the velocities of prices and money. In terms of the model, this implies that the growth rates of the price and of the money supply g_0 and g_1, have to be equal. However, as noted at the beginning of this section, this does not reflect one of the characteristics of hyperinflation, namely a rate of inflation which is higher than the rate of increase in the money supply.

The previous remarks are basically formulated as econometric comments. They may however be put in a different way. As suggested by Malinvaud (1982, Chapter 8), we will now refer to the underlying economic theory. Consider for instance the Cambridge equation. It is essentially derived from a growth theory, i.e. a long-term theory. Consequently, the relations between the growth rates g_0 and g_1 must be seen as relations between long-term rates. On the other hand, hyperinflation is essentially a short-term phenomenon. It follows that the structural models describing this phenomenon should be based on adjustment models and not on long-term models. This confusion between short- and long-term models is the most important source of the unsatisfactory properties emphasized in the previous discussion. To overcome this problem, Malinvaud (1982) has suggested the inclusion of a reduced form price evolution equation in the original specification of the model. In order to have stationary movements, it is preferable to use the inflation rate instead of the log of the price. The resulting equation is:

$$\Delta p_t = a\, E[\Delta p_{t+1} | I_t] + u_t, \qquad (3.4)$$

with $\Delta p_t = p_t - p_{t-1}$ and u_t being a variable summarizing the short-term factors. In terms of resolution, Equation (3.4) is analogous to (3.3), however there are important differences in interpretation. Developing the first-order differences in (3.4) yields:

$$p_t = \frac{a}{1+a} E[p_t | I_{t-1}] + \frac{1}{1+a} p_{t-1} + \frac{u_t}{1+a}.$$

It follows that the equation includes not only a future expectation but also a lagged endogenous term. Note however that the effects of these two variables are linked because of the constraint on the structural parameters: the sum of the corresponding coefficients is equal to 1.

It is also important to note that the meaning of u_t in (3.4) is quite different from the meaning of this term in (3.1). Here the residual term depends on factors explaining the short-term movements of prices. Usually these factors are separated into two classes: factors in the first class correspond to cost modifications (cost inflation), while factors in the second class describe disequilibria between supply and demand (demand inflation). In model (3.1), the factors summarized by the residual variables u_{1t}, u_{2t}, u_{3t}, u_{4t} are implicitly associated with behavioral changes. They do not include, for instance, variables representing disequilibria (such as demand inflation). Intuitively, this would be incompatible with assumptions concerning equilibrium made in specifying model (3.1). In other words, the difficulty comes from the fact that the model does not take into account the possibility of the existence of a long-term equilibrium together with short-term disequilibria.

1.4. The evolution of an asset price

Another classical example of a rational expectations model concerns dynamic asset pricing. Let us at first consider a deterministic framework and denote p_t the unit asset price at time t, d_t the unit dividend for period [t, t+1], and η the discount rate. The dynamic equilibrium condition is:

$$p_t = \frac{1}{1+\eta} p_{t+1} + d_t. \qquad (3.5)$$

It states that the dividend exactly compensates the actualized price difference from one period to the next.

In an uncertain environment, one often specifies, by analogy, a relation of the same type with the future price replaced by its expectation:

$$p_t = \frac{1}{1+\eta} E[p_{t+1}|I_t] + d_t. \qquad (3.6)$$

It is thus implicitly assumed that the dividend d_t and the discount rate η are known at time t. It is also implicitly supposed that the equilibrium condition in an uncertain environment is directly derived from the equilibrium condition given in the deterministic case by replacing the unknown variables — here p_{t+1} — by their (conditional) expectations. This use of the *certainty-equivalent principle* requires some restrictive conditions on the underlying structural model. We will not make this point explicit here. It will be further detailed in Section 6.

2. A description of the solution methods

We start here with a reduced equation which is analogous to the price equations (3.3) and (3.4). However we adopt the following general notations:

y_t is the endogenous variable at time t;
u_t is the summary of all the exogenous factors at time t;
I_t is the information set available at time t.

The basic equation is:

$$y_t = a\, E[y_{t+1}|I_t] + u_t. \tag{3.7}$$

The evolution of the residual term (u_t) is assumed to be given. A *solution* of equation (3.7) is a stochastic process (y_t) compatible with this equation. In order to ensure that the expectation plays a real role in the model, we restrict the reduced parameter a to be different from zero.

As will be shown, Equation (3.7) admits an infinite number of solutions. Among the solution methods proposed in the literature, we will first present those that lead to the determination of particular solutions, and then describe those that give the general solution.

2.1. The "forward" — "backward" approach

The solution method suggested by Blanchard (1979) is based on very intuitive reasoning. It consists of a recursive solution technique. Depending on whether the recursive substitutions are made in a forward or backward — looking approach, the resulting solution is called the forward or backward solution.

a) The forward approach Applying forward recursive substitutions to equation (3.7) yields:

$$\begin{aligned}
y_t &= a\, E[y_{t+1}|I_t] + u_t \\
&= a^2\, E[y_{t+1}|I_t] + u_t + a\, E[u_{t+1}|I_t] \\
&\vdots \\
&= a^i\, E[y_{t+i}|I_t] + u_t + a\, E[u_{t+1}|I_t] + \ldots + a^{i-1}\, E[u_{t+i-1}|I_t].
\end{aligned}$$

If the series of the variables $a^i\, E[u_{t+i}|I_t]$ converges, then equation (3.7) admits the particular solution given by:

$$y_t^F = \sum_{i=0}^{\infty} a^i\, E[u_{t+i}|I_t]. \quad (3.8)$$

For this solution, the current endogenous variable depends on the expectations, formed at time t, of all the future exogenous variables.

The series defining the forward-solution does not always exist. To develop this point, let us consider a residual term (u_t) corresponding to a stationary process. The importance of the general term of the series may be measured by:

$$E[a^i\, E[u_{t+i}|I_t]]^2 = a^{2i}\, E(E[u_{t+i}|I_t])^2$$
$$= a^{2i}\{V(E[u_{t+i}|I_t]) + (E\, E[u_{t+i}|I_t])^2\}$$
$$\leq a^{2i}\{Vu_{t+i} + (E\, u_{t+i})^2\},$$

by using the variance analysis equation (see Section 1). Since (u_t) is a stationary process, the quantity $Vu_{t+i} + (E\, u_{t+i})^2$ is a constant. It follows that, as soon as the coefficient a has a modulus smaller than 1, the series defining the forward solution converges in quadratic mean.

Property (3.9): A sufficient condition for existence of the forward solution is the stationarity of the exogenous process (u_t) with the constraint $|a| < 1$.

For instance, assume that the exogenous process can be represented by an autoregressive model of order 1:

$$u_t = \rho u_{t-1} + \epsilon_t, \quad |\rho| < 1,$$

where (ϵ_t) is an independent white noise, i.e. a sequence of independent variables having the zero mean and same variance. It follows that $u_{t+1} = \rho u_t + \epsilon_{t+1}$. Now suppose that the available information I_t is only composed of the current and past values of u. Then u_t belongs to this information set while ϵ_{t+1} is orthogonal to it. Consequently the optimal forecast of u_{t+1} made with the information set I_t is proportional to u_t:

$$E[u_{t+1}|I_t] = \rho u_t.$$

The same argument may be used for higher order horizons. Recursive substitutions yield:

$$u_{t+i} = \rho^i u_t + \rho^{i-1}\epsilon_{t+1} + \rho^{i-2}\epsilon_{t+2} + \ldots + \epsilon_{t+i},$$

and thus:

$$E[u_{t+i}|I_t] = \rho^i u_t.$$

The forward solution has the following form:

$$y_t^F = \sum_{i=0}^{\infty} a^i \rho^i u_t,$$

or equivalently

$$y_t^F = \frac{1}{1-a\rho} u_t.$$

For this solution, the expectation of the future endogenous variable is:

$$E[y_{t+1}^F | I_t] = \frac{1}{1-a\rho} E[u_{t+1} | I_t] = \frac{\rho u_t}{1-a\rho}.$$

The forward solution has, in some applications, an interesting economic interpretation. Consider for instance equation (3.6) describing the evolution of an asset price. The forward solution leads to the following price sequence:

$$p_t^F = \sum_{i=0}^{\infty} \frac{1}{(1+\eta)^i} E[d_{t+i} | I_t] = E[V_t | I_t], \tag{3.10}$$

where $V_t = \sum_{i=0}^{\infty} \frac{1}{(1+\eta)^i} d_{t+i}$. V_t is the discounted sum of all dividends payed between t and ∞; p_t^F is thus the expectation of this discounted sum, i.e. the present value of the firm.

In the previous example it is interesting to interpret the asymptotic behavior of $1/(1+\eta)^i E[p_{t+i} | I_t]$. If this quantity converges (for $i \to \infty$) toward a strictly positive value, the agents would expect an asymptotic selling price that always remains advantageous. Hence they would be inclined to keep their assets. This would lead to the paradoxal situation in which equilibrium at finite times would become impossible because of the lack of asset suppliers. In such a case of a generation that lives indefinitely, it might seem natural to impose the following condition:

$$\lim_{i \to \infty} \frac{1}{(1+\eta)^i} E[p_{t+i} | I_t] = 0.$$

This condition is often described as the transversality condition associated with an underlying intertemporal optimization problem. When

REDUCED FORMS OF RATIONAL EXPECTATIONS MODELS

this condition is imposed, the forward solution becomes the unique admissible solution.

b) The backward approach To solve equation (3.7) in a backward manner requires an expression of the future variable y_{t+1} in terms of current variables. One thus has to "extract" the realization y_{t+1} out of the expectation $E[y_{t+1}|I_t]$. In practice this is done by examining whether there exists a perfect foresight solution, i.e. a solution such that $y_{t+1} = E[y_{t+1}|I_t]$. When it does exist, equation (3.7) yields:

$$y_t = a\, y_{t+1} + u_t$$

$$\Leftrightarrow y_{t+1} = \frac{1}{a} y_t - \frac{1}{a} u_t$$

$$\Leftrightarrow y_t = \frac{1}{a} y_{t-1} - \frac{1}{a} u_{t-1}.$$

This is an equation without expectations. It may be analysed directly. Carrying out successive substitutions results in the following series:

$$y_t^B = - \sum_{i=1}^{\infty} \frac{1}{a^i} u_{t-i}. \tag{3.11}$$

If Equation (3.11) describes a convergent series, it is a solution to the perfect foresight model associated with equation (3.7). Moreover, it is a solution to Equation (3.7) itself when y_{t+1}^B is perfectly predictable. This condition is met when the available information I_t includes the current and past values of the exogenous variables that affect the residual term u.

Property (3.12): If the series, having a general term $(1/a^i)\, u_{t-i}$ converges (in square mean) and the information set I_t includes u_t, $u_{t-1}, \ldots$ then $y_t^B = - \sum_{i=1}^{\infty} \frac{1}{a^i} u_{t-i}$ is a solution — called the *backward solution* — to the rational expectations model (3.7).

The backward solution may be written in a condensed way by using the lag operator L:

$$y_t^B = - \sum_{i=1}^{\infty} \frac{1}{a^i} L^i u_t = - \frac{L}{a-L} u_t.$$

Suppose now that the exogenous process (u_t) is stationary. It follows that the backward solution exists if and only if the root of the autoregressive part $(a - L)$ has a modulus larger than 1, i.e. if and only if $|a| > 1$. At first sight, the existence domains of the forward and backward solutions seem complementary. However, as will be shown in the next subsection, the forward solution has a wider domain (remember that property (3.9) only gives a sufficient condition for existence).

Finally, note that the backward solution is a very special one (when it does exist) because it is built on the perfect foresight assumption, thus it does not allow for forecast errors. In a stochastic model, this is a very strong restriction on the agents' behavior. To some extent, this solution may be seen as the deterministic limit case of the rational expectations model.

2.2. Linear solutions

a) The evolution of the exogenous process In dynamic models, it is often useful to complete the basic formulation concerning the evolution of the endogenous process by a relation describing the evolution of the exogenous variables. Indeed the initial equation gives the current endogenous variable in terms of lagged endogenous terms and some exogenous variables, but it does not assume anything about either the dynamics of the exogenous process itself, or the specification of the information sets.

Let us focus on the evolution of the exogenous process. When no particular formulation is implied by the economic theory embodied in the model, one frequently retains a descriptive model based on a stationary time-series having an ARMA (autoregressive — moving average) form or on non-stationary time-series having an ARIMA form (i.e. with roots of the autoregressive part equal to 1). These formulations allow for a large range of possible behaviors. In all the cases, the process denoted u may be written as a weighted average of the current and lagged components of its innovations. More precisely, we have:

$$u_t = \sum_{j=0}^{\infty} h_j \epsilon_{t-j}, \qquad (3.13)$$

where (ϵ_t) is an independent white noise vector having a size equal to the number (denoted p) of exogenous variables that are taken into account in the underlying structural model. The coefficients h_j, $j = 0 \ldots \infty$, are row — vectors of size $1 \times p$.

Formulation (3.13) makes sense if the coefficients h_j are such that:

$$\sum_{j=0}^{\infty} h_j h_j' < \infty,$$ where the symbol ' means transposition. With this condition satisfied, the process u defined by (3.13) is stationary. To extend the presentation to non-stationary processes, i.e. to cases where

$$\sum_{j=0}^{\infty} h_j h_j' = \infty,$$ it is sufficient to make a choice of initial values. For instance, one can take zero values for the noise before an initial date $t = 0$ and then obtain:

$$u_t = \sum_{j=0}^{t} h_j \epsilon_{t-j} = \sum_{j=0}^{\infty} h_j \tilde{\epsilon}_{t-j}, \qquad (3.14)$$

with $\tilde{\epsilon}_t = \begin{cases} \epsilon_t, & \text{for } t \geq 0, \\ 0, & \text{for } t < 0. \end{cases}$

With these restrictions, one gets a non-stationary process. In particular, Formula (3.14) incorporates the case of ARMA processes with initial conditions set at zero.

The previous moving-average formulations may also be summarized with the use of the lag-operator L. Equation (3.14) becomes:

$$u_t = h(L)\tilde{\epsilon}_t, \text{ where } h(L) = \sum_{j=0}^{\infty} h_j L^j. \qquad (3.15)$$

b) Determination of the linear solutions In addition to the ARMA or ARIMA representation of the exogenous process, we assume here that the information set available at time t is composed of the past and current exogenous variables. Equivalently, it can be taken as being composed of the past and current innovations.

Since the information set is now precisely specified, it is possible to make explicit the derivation of the expectations. For instance, in the case of a non-stationary process with zero values before the initial date, the expected innovations are given by:

$$E[\tilde{\epsilon}_{t+j} | I_t] = \begin{cases} 0, & \text{for } j > 0 \\ \tilde{\epsilon}_{t+j}, & \text{for } j \leq 0. \end{cases}$$

We can now go back to model (3.7) and examine whether it has solutions with a structure analogous to that chosen for the residual term u. In other words, we look for solutions of Equation (3.7) that can be written as:

$$y_t = C(L)\,\tilde{\epsilon}_t,$$

where $C(L) = \sum_{j=0}^{\infty} c_j L^j$ is an operator that has to be determined. The coefficients denoted c_j measure the effects on y_{t+j} of shocks affecting the current exogenous variables. These shocks are transmitted through the innovations [see Sims (1980)].

Let us now compute the expectations of the desired linear solutions. First, observe that the future endogenous variable may be written as:

$$y_{t+1} = C(L)\tilde{\epsilon}_{t+1} = c_0\,\tilde{\epsilon}_{t+1} + \frac{C(L)-c_0}{L}\tilde{\epsilon}_t,$$

Then, using the formula giving the expected innovations, one obtains:

$$E[y_{t+1}|I_t] = c_0 E[\tilde{\epsilon}_{t+1}|I_t] + E\left[\frac{C(L)-c_0}{L}\tilde{\epsilon}_t\,\Big|\,I_t\right]$$

$$= \frac{C(L)-c_0}{L}\tilde{\epsilon}_t.$$

Replacing the expectation in Equation (3.7) by this expression yields:

$$y_t = a\,E[y_{t+1}|I_t] + u_t$$

$$\Leftrightarrow C(L)\tilde{\epsilon}_t = a\,\frac{C(L)-c_0}{L}\tilde{\epsilon}_t + h(L)\tilde{\epsilon}_t.$$

If strict multicollinearity does not exist among the exogenous variables of the model, then the components of the noise are not linearly linked and a term-by-term identification may be performed to give:

$$C(L) = a\,\frac{C(L)-c_0}{L} + h(L),$$

$$\Leftrightarrow C(L)(L-a) = -a\,c_0 + L\,h(L)$$

$$\Leftrightarrow C(L) = -\frac{ac_0}{L-a} + L\,\frac{h(L)}{L-a}.$$

The solution method that has been followed is actually the undetermined coefficients procedure suggested for instance by Muth (1961) and Mac Callum (1976). Note that the use of lag operator polynomials greatly simplifies the technical derivations.

The linear solutions are characterized by the moving-average operator C(L). They depend not only on the evolution of the exogenous process [h(L)], on the structural parameter of the conditional model [a], but also on p auxiliary parameters, components of the row-vector c_0. Consequently there exists an infinite number of such solutions.

Property (3.16): Consider the following rational expectations model:

$$y_t = a\, E[y_{t+1}|I_t] + u_t.$$

If the exogenous process verifies:

$$u_t = h(L)\tilde{\epsilon}_t,$$

and the information set available at time t is given by:

$$I_t = \{\tilde{\epsilon}_t, \tilde{\epsilon}_{t-1}, \tilde{\epsilon}_{t-2}, \ldots\},$$

then the model has an infinity of linear solutions written as:

$$y_t = \left[-\frac{a c_0}{L-a} + \frac{L\, h(L)}{L-a} \right] \tilde{\epsilon}_t, \quad c_0 \in R^p.$$

c) The role of the backward solution The linear solutions have been obtained under the condition that the innovations are equal to zero before the initial date $t = 0$. In this framework, the backward solution always exists. It is given by:

$$y_t^B = \frac{-L}{a-L} u_t = \frac{L\, h(L)}{L-a} \tilde{\epsilon}_t.$$

This expression clearly shows that the linear solutions described by Property (3.16) may be written as:

$$y_t = -\frac{a c_0}{L-a} \tilde{\epsilon}_t + y_t^B.$$

The first term includes the current exogenous innovation, while the backward solution only includes past values of $\tilde{\epsilon}$.

The linear solutions constitute an affine space containing the backward solution. The dimension of this space is equal to p, which denotes the number of exogenous variables of the underlying structural model.

d) Linear stationary solutions Stationarity will be introduced as a limit case of the previous approach. We will first assume that the exogenous process is stationary and then search for the linear stationary solutions. As will be shown, further restrictions need to be imposed to the solutions obtained above.

Consider an exogenous process admitting the following representation:

$$u_t = \sum_{j=0}^{\infty} h_j \epsilon_{t-j},$$

with $\sum_{j=0}^{\infty} h_j h_j' < \infty$.

We now investigate whether any of the previously obtained linear solutions exhibit stationary behavior. For this purpose, we must discuss the convergence of the series $\sum_{j=0}^{\infty} c_j c_j'$. Since the c_j's are the coefficients of the development of the following operator:

$$C(L) = \frac{1}{a-L}[-a c_0 + L h(L)],$$

it appears that two cases must be distinguished.

First case: $|a| > 1$ The moving-average development of $1/(a-L)$ always leads to a convergent series. Therefore whatever the value of c_0, the linear solutions are asymptotically stationary.

Second case: $|a| \leq 1$ The development of $1/(a-L)$ always corresponds to a divergent series. The condition $\sum_{j=0}^{\infty} c_j c_j' < \infty$ will only be satisfied when the coefficient a is also a root of the numerator $-a c_0 + L h(L)$. Otherwise the explosive denominator may not be neutralized and stationarity is impossible. Consequently, the only admissible choice for the auxiliary parameter is:

$$c_0 = h(a).$$

Among all linear solutions, one is stationary and corresponds to:

$$C(L) = \frac{1}{a-L}(-a\,h(a) + L\,h(L)).$$

The following property summarizes the preceding analysis.

Property (3.17): Consider the following rational expectations model:

$$y_t = a\,E[y_{t+1}|I_t] + u_t.$$

If the stationary exogenous process is defined by:

$$u_t = h(L)\epsilon_t,$$

and the information set at time t is given by:

$$I_t = \{\epsilon_t, \epsilon_{t-1}, \epsilon_{t-2}, \ldots\},$$

then:

a) If $|a| > 1$, the model has an infinity of linear stationary solutions written as:

$$y_t = \left(-\frac{a\,c_0}{a-L} + \frac{L\,h(L)}{a-L}\right)\epsilon_t,\ c_0 \in R^P.$$

b) If $|a| \le 1$, the model has a unique linear stationary solution written as:

$$y_t = \left(\frac{L\,h(L) - a\,h(a)}{a-L}\right)\epsilon_t.$$

e) A robust solution   When $|a| < 1$, the sufficient condition given by property (3.9) is fulfilled. Consequently, in this case the existence of the forward solution is ensured. Furthermore it is the unique linear stationary solution[1]:

$$y_t^F = \frac{L\,h(L) - a\,h(a)}{a-L}\epsilon_t.$$

On the other hand, when $|a| > 1$, this solution also exists because it corresponds to a precise choice of c_0, namely $c_0 = h(a)$, which is

---

[1] For a formal proof of this assertion see for instance Gouriéoux, Laffont and Monfort (1982).

obviously admissible. However, the forward-looking representation of this solution fails since the series no longer exists.

Thus this solution plays a very special role: it is the only linear stationary solution that exists for all values of the structural parameter a. This robustness property has sometimes been overstated by taking this solution as equivalent to the model itself. Such an assertion is generally invalid. Strong restrictions on the model would be needed to preclude all the other solutions. It remains evident that the "forward" solution has a privileged status, especially when $|a| < 1$.

2.3. The general solution

a) The homogeneous equation approach Except for the expectation term, the model described in this section looks like a linear difference equation. The method introduced by Gouriéroux, Laffont and Monfort (1982) starts from this observation. It applies to the rational expectations model a solution technique analogous to the technique that is traditionally used for difference equations. More precisely, the general solution is obtained by a two-step procedure. The first step involves the determination of a particular solution. The second step corresponds to the resolution of the associated homogeneous equation.

Let (y_t^0) be a particular solution to Equation (3.7) and take another solution (y_t) to the same equation. The two following relations then hold simultaneously:

$$\begin{cases} y_t = a\, E[y_{t+1}|I_t] + u_t, \\ y_t^0 = a\, E[y_{t+1}^0|I_t] + u_t. \end{cases}$$

We substract the second relation from the first and use the linearity property of the conditional expectation operator to get:

$$z_t = a\, E[z_{t+1}|I_t],$$

where $z_t = y_t - y_t^0$ denotes the difference between the two solutions. The stochastic process (z_t) thus also satisfies a rational expectation equation. However, this equation appears to be homogeneous, i.e. it corresponds to a zero residual term.

The homogeneous equation is equivalent to:

$$a^t z_t = E[a^{t+1} z_{t+1}|I_t].$$

Consequently the process $(M_t = a^t z_t)$ is such that the rational expectation $E[M_{t+1}|I_t]$ coincides with the naive one M_t. As defined in Section 1, this property is characteristic of martingales. The described procedure leads to the following property.

Property (3.18): If (y_t^0) is a particular solution to model (3.7), then all the other solutions are given by:

$$y_t = y_t^0 + \frac{1}{a^t} M_t.$$

b) The approach based on prediction errors Another way to obtain the general solution has been proposed by Broze, Gouriéroux and Szafarz (1985). This method implicitly appeared in some earlier works (Pesaran (1981), Gouriéroux, Laffont and Monfort (1982)). It has the advantage of being easily generalizable to models having a more general structure than Equation (3.7) (see Section 4).

The basic idea is inspired by the backward solution approach. The latter only leads to a particular solution because of the perfect foresight assumption that has been introduced. Here, this restriction is avoided and the prediction error made explicit. More precisely, for any process (y_t), the realization at time $t+1$ can be expressed by means of the expectation made at time t and the corresponding prediction error denoted ϵ_{t+1}^0:

$$y_{t+1} = E[y_{t+1}|I_t] + \epsilon_{t+1}^0.$$

Since expectations are rationally formed, the process (ϵ_t^0) has to fulfill the characteristic property of a rational prediction error. In other words, ϵ_t^0 has to be orthogonal to the past:

$$E[\epsilon_t^0|I_{t-1}] = 0, \forall t.$$

On the other hand, ϵ_t^0 is obviously included in I_t since the information set increases and contains y_t. It follows that the process (ϵ_t^0) is a martingale difference.

Let us now consider the model:

$$y_t = a E[y_{t+1}|I_t] + u_t.$$

The expectation may be replaced by using the prediction error:

$$y_t = a(y_{t+1} - \epsilon_{t+1}^0) + u_t.$$

An equivalent form is given by:

$$y_t = \frac{1}{a} y_{t-1} - \frac{1}{a} u_{t-1} + \epsilon_t^0.$$

This equation describes the solution of Equation (3.7). The only remaining problem concerns the possible choices of the prediction error. The following property gives an answer to this problem.

Property (3.19):

a) Any solution y to Equation (3.7) satisfies the following difference equation:

$$y_t = \frac{1}{a} y_{t-1} - \frac{1}{a} u_{t-1} + \epsilon_t^0.$$

where ϵ_t^0 denotes the prediction error.

b) Conversely, if ϵ_t^0 is an arbitrary martingale difference and y is a solution to the previous difference equation, then y is a solution to Equation (3.7).

Proof The first part has been proved in the text. In order to establish the second part, we take the conditional expectation of both sides of the difference equation with respect to the information set I_{t-1}:

$$E[y_t | I_t] = \frac{1}{a} y_{t-1} - \frac{1}{a} u_{t-1} + E[\epsilon_t^0 | I_{t-1}]$$

$$\frac{1}{a} y_{t-1} - \frac{1}{a} u_{t-1}.$$

The transition from the first line to the second is a consequence of the assumption that ϵ_t^0, as a martingale difference, is orthogonal to the past information.

We now subtract side by side the previous expression from the difference equation and obtain:

$$\epsilon_t^0 = y_t - E[y_t | I_{t-1}].$$

This shows that the arbitrarily chosen martingale difference is necessarily equal to the error made in predicting the endogenous process y.

Replacing ϵ_t^0 by its expression in the difference equation yields:

$$y_t = \frac{1}{a} y_{t-1} - \frac{1}{a} u_{t-1} + y_t - E[y_t | I_{t-1}]$$

or equivalently:

$$y_{t-1} = a\,E[y_t | I_{t-1}] + u_{t-1}.$$

The latter exactly corresponds to Equation (3.7) written for the lagged endogenous variable.

QED

In conclusion, the approach based on prediction errors provides a direct method for eliminating the expectation term in the original model.

3. Properties of the solution set

3.1. Impact of a terminal condition

Suppose that the endogenous variable is known at a given date t_0. It follows from Equation (3.7) that:

$$y_{t_0-1} = a\,E[y_{t_0} | I_{t_0-1}] + u_{t_0-1}.$$

The endogenous variable at time $t_0 - 1$ is unambiguously determined since the exogenous variable and y_{t_0} are known. Step by step, the same argument applies to every date before t_0. The knowledge of y_{t_0} thus fixes all past values of the endogenous process: $y_{t_0-1}, y_{t_0-2}, \ldots$. A terminal condition leads to the determination of a unique solution (since t_0 is viewed as a terminal date, we only pay attention to the dates that precede t_0).

3.2. Impact of an initial condition

Again assume a known value for y_{t_0}. We now examine the behavior of the endogenous process after t_0. With the use of the prediction error approach, we have:

$$y_{t_0+1} = \frac{1}{a} y_{t_0} - \frac{1}{a} u_{t_0} + \epsilon^0_{t_0+1},$$

where $\epsilon^0_{t_0+1}$ is an arbitrary variable orthogonal to the information set I_{t_0}. To any admissible $\epsilon^0_{t_0+1}$ corresponds a possible value y_{t_0+1}. In consequence, there exists an infinite number of future values y_{t_0+1} compatible with the value given for time t_0.

Consider the next value y_{t_0+2}. Following the same method we obtain:

$$y_{t_0+2} = \frac{1}{a} y_{t_0+1} - \frac{1}{a} u_{t_0+1} + \epsilon^0_{t_0+2}$$

$$= \frac{1}{a^2} y_{t_0} - \frac{1}{a} u_{t_0+1} - \frac{1}{a^2} u_{t_0} + \epsilon^0_{t_0+2} + \frac{1}{a} \epsilon^0_{t_0+1}.$$

The non-uniqueness property is now reflected by two arbitrary variables, $\epsilon^0_{t_0+1}$ and $\epsilon^0_{t_0+2}$, that are orthogonal to I_{t_0} and I_{t_0+1}, respectively.

The multiplicity of solutions grows with time (after t_0). For a given y_{t_0}, the evolution of the multiplicity may be intuitively represented as shown on Figure 7.

Note that this phenomenon is specific to rational expectations models. It does not occur in deterministic models or even in the perfect foresight version of our model. The latter is given by:

$$y_t = a\, y_{t+1} + u_t.$$

In such a case, it is well-known that knowledge of y_{t_0} is sufficient for determining all values of the endogenous process. Past and future values have, in this respect, exactly the same status. In other words, in a random environment, rationality introduces an asymmetry

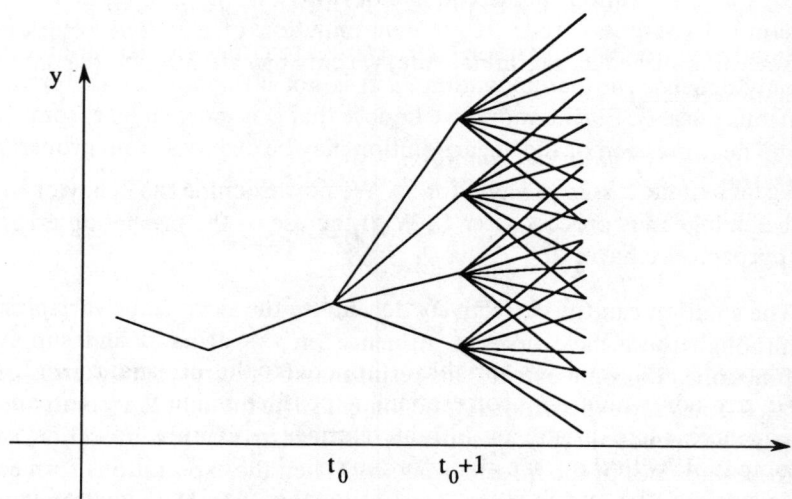

FIGURE 7

between the past and future: past values are known for sure while future values are only (optimally) predicted.

3.3. Sunspots

Till now, we have often chosen as the information set the set generated by the current and past values of the exogenous variables entering the underlying structural model. It is also possible to enlarge the information set and include, for instance, sunspots.

In our terminology, *sunspots* are variables independent from the exogenous variables that influence the demand and supply functions. They are extraneous to the original structural model. However, as will be shown, their presence in the information sets can affect the evolution of the endogenous process.

To simplify the presentation, we will restrict ourselves to the linear solutions of model (3.7). Sunspots may be introduced by means of a white noise process ($\tilde{\epsilon}_{2t}$) distinct from the innovation ($\tilde{\epsilon}_{1t}$) of the exogenous process. We thus assume that:

$$I_t = \{\tilde{\epsilon}_t, \tilde{\epsilon}_{t-1}, \ldots\}$$

where $\tilde{\epsilon}_t = (\tilde{\epsilon}_{1t}, \tilde{\epsilon}_{2t})$, $\forall t$,
and:

$$u_t = h(L)\tilde{\epsilon}_t = h_1(L)\tilde{\epsilon}_{1t} + h_2(L)\tilde{\epsilon}_{2t} = h_1(L)\tilde{\epsilon}_{1t}.$$

In other words, the condition $h_2(L) = 0$ says that the residual variable u_t only depends on the innovation $\tilde{\epsilon}_1$. It is not influenced by the extraneous noise $\tilde{\epsilon}_2$. Furthermore, we impose that $\tilde{\epsilon}_2$ is independent from $\tilde{\epsilon}_1$.

The expression of the linear solution may be deduced from property (3.16):

$$y_t = \left[\frac{-a c_0^1}{L-a}\tilde{\epsilon}_{1t} + \frac{L h_1(L)}{L-a}\tilde{\epsilon}_{1t}\right] + \frac{-a c_0^2}{L-a}\tilde{\epsilon}_{2t}.$$

The solution can thus effectively depend on the extraneous variables, although these have no real influence on the demand and supply functions. To some extent, this result may be interpreted in terms of "self-fulfilling expectations" phenomena. The thought that some sunspots influence the price sequence will lead to the incorporation of these variables in the information sets. Then the expectations formed with the use of these sets will reflect the presence of the extraneous variables. Since expectations influence the price itself, the whole price path will be submitted to a real effect of the sunspots. This will reassure the agents in their belief that sunspots play a crucial role in price determination.

Moreover, the independence assumption leads to:

$$V y_t = V \left[\frac{-a c_0^1}{L-a} \tilde{\epsilon}_{1t} + \frac{L h_1(L)}{L-a} \tilde{\epsilon}_{1t} \right] + V \left[\frac{a c_0^2}{L-a} \tilde{\epsilon}_{2t} \right]$$

$$\geq V \left[\frac{-a c_0^1}{L-a} \tilde{\epsilon}_{1t} + \frac{L h_1(L)}{L-a} \tilde{\epsilon}_{1t} \right].$$

Taking into account extraneous variables gives a larger variability to the solution. This kind of inequality may be used to test for the presence of sunspots. It is especially interesting in financial theory where sunspots can be interpreted in terms of excess volatility [see Shiller (1979, 1981), Leroy and Porter (1981)]. Nevertheless, the role of sunspots and self-fulfilling expectations on the one hand, and speculative bubbles on the other hand, has not yet been fully elucidated [see Leroy (1984), Adam and Szafarz (1987)].

3.4. Stationary solutions

We have previously analyzed the set of the linear stationary solutions of Equation (3.7). It has been pointed out that two cases are to be distinguished according to the value taken by the modulus of the structural parameter a. In this subsection we intend to stress the non-uniqueness problem that arises when $|a| > 1$.

To put the problem in a simple fashion, we here assume that $|a| > 1$ and that u is an independent white noise (with identically distributed components). Let us consider a mapping f such that $f(u_t)$ admits second order moments and define the process ϵ^0 as:

$$\epsilon_t^0 = f(u_t) - E f(u_t).$$

This process obviously has independent, identically distributed components. Furthermore it is a martingale difference. Then from property (3.19), the following relation provides solutions to Equation (3.7):

$$y_t = \frac{1}{a} y_{t-1} - \frac{1}{a} u_{t-1} + f(u_t) - E f(u_t).$$

Recursive substitutions yield:

$$y_t = \sum_{j=0}^{\infty} \frac{1}{a^j} \left[-\frac{u_{t-j-1}}{a} + f(u_{t-j}) - Ef(u_{t-j}) \right].$$

This formula describes stationary solutions that are generally non-linear. Linear stationary solutions only occur for choices of a linear mapping f.

This remark shows how severe non-uniqueness may be. Whatever the value of a, the model has a non-parametrizable set of solutions. In the case $|a| > 1$, the model still has a non-parametrizable set of stationary solutions. However the additional assumption of linearity leads to a parameterizable set. This set appears much more tractable for further developments, whether empirical or analytical.

3.5. *Variability of the linear stationary solutions*

We consider the case $|a| > 1$ together with the minimal information sequence (i.e. no sunspots). There exists an infinity of linear stationary solutions given by:

$$y_t = \left[-\frac{ac_0}{L-a} + \frac{Lh(L)}{L-a} \right] \epsilon_t, \text{ with } c_0 \in R^p.$$

Let us now introduce the following processes:

$$y_t^0 = \frac{Lh(L)}{L-a} \epsilon_t,$$

and

$$y_t^j = -\frac{a}{L-a} \epsilon_{jt}, \quad j=1,\ldots,p,$$

where ϵ_{jt} denotes the jth component of ϵ_t. The linear stationary solutions may then be rewritten as:

$$y_t = \sum_{j=1}^{p} c_{0j} y_t^j + y_t^0,$$

where c_{0j} is the jth component of the row-vector c_0. The coefficients c_{0j} may be arbitrarily chosen. We will henceforth examine whether there exist particular values of these coefficients that would lead to the minimal variability solution [see Taylor (1977)].

Since we have restricted the analysis to solutions that are combinations of current and past values of the noise ϵ, the sequences y^0 and y^j, $j=1\ldots p$, are centered and the minimization problem becomes:

$$\operatorname*{Min}_{c_{0j}} E[y_t]^2 = E\left(y_t^0 + \sum_{j=1}^{p} c_{0j} y_t^j\right)^2.$$

In this form, the problem appears as the classical (theoretical) least squares problem. Consequently, it has a unique solution. The optimal choice for the coefficients is provided by the values opposite to the regression coefficients of y_t^0 on y_t^j, $j=1\ldots p$:

$$\begin{pmatrix} \hat{c}_1 \\ \hat{c}_2 \\ \vdots \\ \hat{c}_p \end{pmatrix} = - \begin{pmatrix} Vy_t^1 & \cdots\cdots & \operatorname{Cov}(y_t^1, y_t^p) \\ \cdot & Vy_t^2 & \cdots & \cdot \\ \cdot & \cdots\cdots & \cdot \\ \operatorname{Cov}(y_t^p, y_t^1) & \cdots\cdots & Vy_t^p \end{pmatrix}^{-1} \begin{pmatrix} \operatorname{Cov}(y_t^0, y_t^1) \\ \operatorname{Cov}(y_t^0, y_t^2) \\ \cdots \\ \operatorname{Cov}(y_t^0, y_t^p) \end{pmatrix}.$$

The minimum variance solution is given by:

$$\hat{y}_t = y_t^0 + \sum_{j=1}^{p} \hat{c}_{0j} y_t^j.$$

The value $\hat{y}_t$ is interpreted as the residual of the preceding regression. It is thus orthogonal to all the variables y_t^j, $j=1,\ldots p$.

Any other linear stationary solution may of course be written as:

$$y_t = \hat{y}_t + \sum_{j=1}^{p} (c_{0j} - \hat{c}_{0j}) y_t^j.$$

The variance of this is:

$$Vy_t = V\hat{y}_t + (c_0 - \hat{c}_0)' Vy_t (c_0 - \hat{c}_0)$$

where $c_0 = (c_{01}, \ldots, c_{0p})'$, $\hat{c}_0 = (\hat{c}_{01}, \ldots, \hat{c}_{0p})'$ and

$$Vy_t = \begin{pmatrix} Vy_t^1 & \cdots\cdots & \operatorname{Cov}(y_t^1, y_t^p) \\ \cdot & Vy_t^2 & \cdots & \cdot \\ \cdot & \cdots\cdots & \cdot \\ \operatorname{Cov}(y_t^p, y_t^1) & \cdots\cdots & Vy_t^p \end{pmatrix}.$$

In particular, this result may be applied to the solution corresponding to $c_0 = 0$ (the backward solution):

$$Vy_t^B = V\hat{y}_t + \hat{c}_0' Vy_t \, \hat{c}_0.$$

Thus, with reference to the backward solution, the general formula for the variance of any linear stationary solution becomes:

$$Vy_t = (Vy_t^B - \hat{c}_0' Vy_t \, \hat{c}_0) + (c_0 - \hat{c}_0)' Vy_t(c_0 - \hat{c}_0). \qquad (3.20)$$

Equation (3.20) provides a decomposition of the variability into two terms: the first term is the minimal variability and the second one is the deviation from this minimal variability.

A priori, it seems reasonable to accord a special status to the solution denoted $\hat{y}$. It corresponds to the intuition that agents predict future values in such a way that the corresponding solution is the less erratic one. The choice of this solution could be compatible with a "no bubble" assumption (in the case $|a| > 1$).

Indeed, all the other linear stationary solutions have a larger variability. Along these lines, the additional term $(c_0 - \hat{c}_0)' Vy_t(c_0 - \hat{c}_0)$ could be viewed as a measure of the size of the corresponding bubble. Nevertheless this argument only makes sense when the structural parameter is such that $|a| > 1$ and when no sunspots are introduced, which is not the usual situation in the "bubble" literature. Therefore the minimum variability criterion has not yet found convincing applications.

4. Learning processes

In Section 2 (subsection 3), we have described a very simple learning process that may be used to evaluate the relevance of the rational expectation hypothesis as a limiting case. In this framework, the agents are assumed to use a naive revision scheme to update their expectations. Actually, this scheme is very crude. Also, it implicitly assumes that a very long time occurs between two successive updatings.

A more sophisticated approach (Bray and Savin (1986), Fourgeaud, Gouriéroux and Pradel (1986), Kiefer (1988a, b), Marcet and Sargent (1986, 1988)) consists in assuming that the agents are "learning" with the use of a regression model. When applied to the hyperinflation model given by Equation (3.7), the procedure may be summarized as follows.

— The "true model", i.e. $y_t = a \tilde{y}_{t+1} + u_t$ (where $\tilde{y}_{t+1}$ denotes the expectations of y_{t+1}), is not known by the learning agents.

— The agents build their predictions on the basis of a regression model (called the "misspecified auxiliary model") with an observable instrumental variable denoted x (chosen one-dimensional for simplicity): $y_\tau = \alpha x_{\tau-1} + \epsilon_\tau$.

— At the beginning of period t, the observed variables are $y_1, \ldots, y_{t-1}, x_0, x_1, \ldots x_t$. The prediction of y_{t+1} is then given by:

$$\tilde{y}_{t+1} = \hat{\alpha}_t x_t, \qquad (3.21)$$

where $\hat{\alpha}_t = \dfrac{\sum_{\tau=1}^{t-1} y_\tau x_{\tau-1}}{\sum_{\tau=1}^{t-1} x_{\tau-1}^2}$.

— According to the "true" model the current of value y_t is then given by:

$$y_t = a \hat{\alpha}_t x_t + u_t. \qquad (3.22)$$

— At the beginning of period $t+1$, the agents rebuild their predictions by using the regression model:

$$\tilde{y}_{t+2} = \hat{\alpha}_{t+1} x_{t+1}. \qquad (3.23)$$

Thanks to (3.22), $\hat{\alpha}_{t+1}$ may be expressed as a revised estimate of $\hat{\alpha}_t$ by the following formula:

$$\hat{\alpha}_{t+1} = \dfrac{\sum_{\tau=1}^{t-1} x_{\tau-1}^2 + a x_t x_{t-1}}{\sum_{\tau=1}^{t} x_{\tau-1}^2} \hat{\alpha}_t + \dfrac{u_t x_{t-1}}{\sum_{\tau=1}^{t} x_{\tau-1}^2}. \qquad (3.24)$$

The previous procedure describes the behavior of the learning agents. The problem is now to know whether the learning process converges toward rationality. At this level, it is required to specify the relation existing between the instrumental variable x and the exogenous variable u appearing in the "true" model. Fourgeaud, Gouriéroux and Pradel (1986) assume that the following stationary relations hold:

$$u_{t+1} = cx_t + v_{t+1}, \text{ with } c = \frac{E(u_{t+1}x_t)}{E(x_t^2)}, E(v_{t+1}x_t) = 0, \quad (3.25)$$

$$x_{t+1} = rx_t + w_{t+1}, \text{ with } r = \frac{E(u_{t+1}x_t)}{E(x_t^2)}, E(w_{t+1}x_t) = 0, \quad (3.26)$$

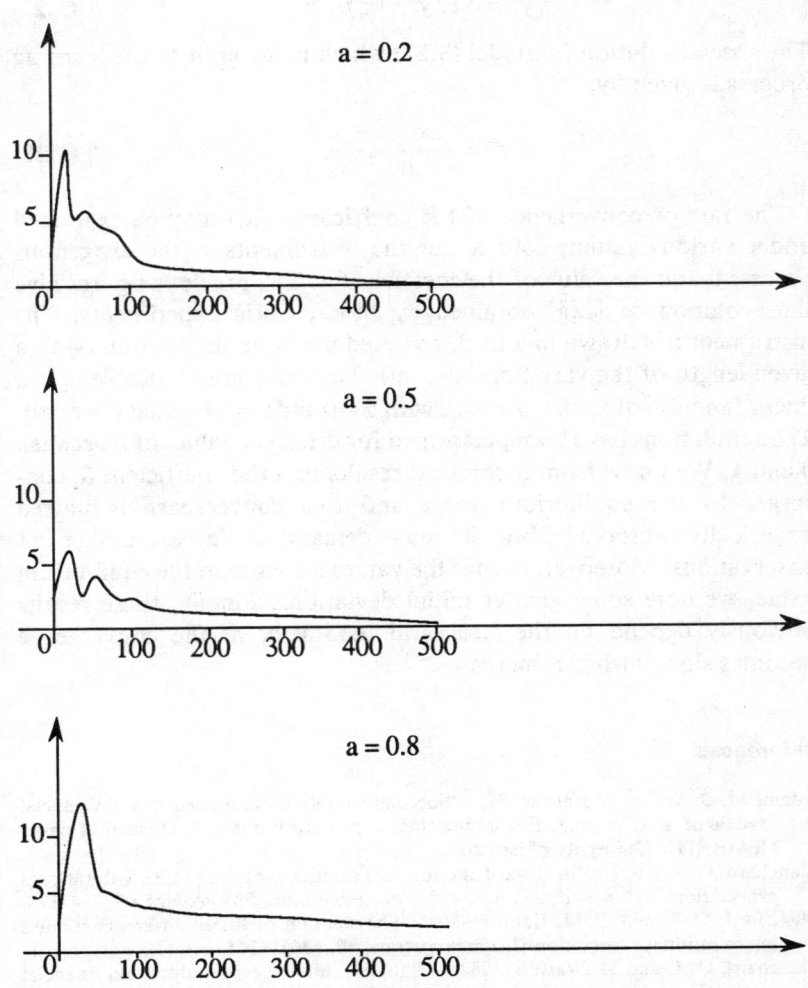

FIGURE 8

Under these assumptions (and some standard regularity conditions), the authors have proved that, if $|a| > 1$, the sequence $(\hat{\alpha}_t)$ converges to $c/(1 - ar)$ for any initial value. Also, the sequence (y_t) generated by the "true model" — together with the expectation scheme (3.21) — tends in probability to a special solution of the corresponding rational expectation model:

$$y_t^* = a\, E[y_{t+1}^* | x_t] + u_t. \qquad (3.27)$$

The special solution to model (3.27) which is the limit to the learning process is given by:

$$y_t^* = \frac{a\,c}{1 - ar} x_t + u_t. \qquad (3.28)$$

The rate of convergence of the coefficients $(\hat{\alpha}_t)$ may be examined under various assumptions about the instruments x, the exogenous process u and the value of the coefficient a. The previous figures give the evolution of $\|\hat{\alpha}_t\|^2$ obtained by Monte-Carlo experiments. The instrument x is drawn in a i.i.d. centered uniform distribution (with a given length of the variation interval). The exogenous variable u_t is a linear function of x_t: $u_t = \mu + v\, x_t$, with $\mu = 0$ and $v = 1$ (so that $c = r = 0$). The simulations have been performed for different values of a between 0 and 1. We know from theoretical results that the coefficient $\hat{\alpha}_t$ converges to the equilibrium value and this convergence is indeed empirically observed, but it may demand a large number of observations. Moreover, even if the values are close to the equilibrium value, we note some greater initial deviations. Finally, these results obviously depend on the structural parameter a: the convergence becomes slower when a increases.

References

Adam, M. C. and A. Szafarz (1987): "Speculative bubbles in monetary and financial models of asset pricing: Evaluating their explanatory power", Discussion paper CEME 8712, University of Brussels.

Blanchard, O. J. (1979): "Backward and forward solutions for economies with rational expectations", *American Economic Review, Papers and Proceedings*, **69**, 114–118.

Blanchard, O. J. and C. M. Kahn (1980): "The solution of linear difference models under rational expectations", *Econometrica*, **48**, 1305–1311.

Blanchard, O. J. and M. Watson (1982): "Bubbles, rational expectations and financial markets", in *Crises in the Economic and Financial Structure*, P. Wachtel (ed.), Lexington Books.

Bray, M. and N. Savin (1986): "Rational expectations equilibria, learning and model specification", *Econometrica*, **54**, 1129-1160.
Broze, L. C. Gouriéroux and A. Szafarz (1985): "Solutions of dynamic linear rational expectations models", *Econometric Theory*, **1**, 341-368.
Burmeister, E., R. Flood and P. Garber (1983): "On the equivalence of solutions in rational expectations models", *Journal of Economic Dynamics and Control*, **5**, 311-321.
Cagan, P. (1956): "The monetary dynamics of hyperinflation", in *Studies in the Quantity Theory of Money*, M. Friedman (ed.), Chicago University Press.
Chow, C. (1980): "Econometric policy evaluation and optimization under rational expectations", *Journal of Economic Dynamics and Control*, **2**, 47-59.
Diba, B. T. and H. I. Grossman (1988): "The theory of rational bubbles in stock prices", *The Economic Journal*, **98**, 746-754.
Evans, G. (1986): "Selection criteria for models with non-uniqueness", *Journal of Monetary Economics*, **18**, 147-157.
Feldman, M. (1987a): "An example of convergence to rational expectations with heterogenous beliefs", *International Economic Review*, **28**, 635-650.
Feldman, M. (1987b): "Bayesian learning and convergence to rational expectations", *Journal of Mathematical Economics*, **16**, 297-313.
Flood, R. P. and P. Garber (1980): "Market fundamentals versus price-level bubbles: The first test", *Journal of Political Economy*, **8**, 745-770.
Fourgeaud, C., C. Gouriéroux and J. Pradel (1986): "Learning procedures and convergence to rationality", *Econometrica*, **54**, 845-868.
Gouriéroux, C., J. J. Laffont and A. Monfort (1982): "Rational expectations in dynamic linear models: analysis of the solutions", *Econometrica*, **50**, 409-425.
Hansen, L. and T. Sargent (1980): "Formulating and estimating linear rational expectations models", *Journal of Economic Dynamics and Control*, **2**, 7-46.
Kiefer, N. (1988a): "Optimal collection of information by partially informed agents", Discussion Paper, Cornell University.
Kiefer, N. (1988b): "A value function arising in the economics information", Discussion Paper, Cornell University.
Leroy, S. (1984): "Efficiency and variability of asset prices", *American Economic Review*, **74**, 183-187.
Leroy, S. and R. Porter (1981): "The present-value relation: Tests based on implied variance bounds", *Econometrica*, **49**, 555-574.
Lucas, R. (1973): "Some international evidence on output inflation trade-offs", *American Economic Review*, **63**, 326-364.
MacCallum, B. T. (1976): "Rational expectations and the estimation of econometric models: an alternative procedure", *International Economic Review*, **17**, 484-490.
MacCallum, B. T. (1983): "On non-uniqueness in rational expectations models: an attempt at perspective", *Journal of Monetary Economics*, **11**, 134-168.
Malinvaud, E. (1982): *Théorie macroéconomique*, Dunod.
Marcet and Sargent (1986): "Convergence of least squares learning mechanisms in self referential linear stochastic models", Federal Reserve Bank, Minneapolis.
Marcet and Sargent (1988): "Least squares learning and the dynamics of hyperinflation", in *Economic Complexity: Chaos, Sunspots, Bubbles and Nonlinearity*, W. Barnett, J. Geweke and K. Shell (eds), Cambridge University Press.
Muth, J. F. (1961) "Rational expectations and the theory of price movements", *Econometrica*, **29**, 315-335.
Pesaran, M. (1981): Solution of linear rational expectations models", *Journal of Econometrics*, **16**, 375-398.
Pesaran, M. (1985): *The Limits to Rational Expectations*, Basil Blackwell, Oxford.

Sargent, T. (1979): *Macroeconomic Theory*, Academic Press, New York.
Sargent, T. and N. Wallace (1973a): "Rational expectations and the dynamics of hyperinflation", *International Economic Review*, **14**, 328-350.
Sargent, T. and N. Wallace (1973b): "The stability of models of money and growth with perfect foresight", *Econometrica*, **41**, 1043-1048.
Sargent, T. and N. Wallace (1975): "Rational expectations, the optimal monetary instruments and the optimal money supply', *Journal of Political Economy*, **83**, 241-254.
Scarth, W. M. (1985): "A note on non-uniqueness in rational expectations models", *Journal of Monetary Economics*, **15**, 247-254.
Sheffrin, S. (1983): *Rational Expectations*, Cambridge University Press.
Shiller, R. (1978): "Rational expectations and the dynamic structure of macroeconomic models", *Journal of Monetary Economics*, **4**, 1-44.
Shiller, R. (1979): "The volatility of long term interest rates and expectations models of the term structure", *Journal of Political Economy*, **87**, 1190-1219.
Shiller, R. (1981): "Do stock prices move too much to be justified by subsequent changes in dividends?", *American Economic Review*, **71**, 421-436.
Sims, C. A. (1980): "Macroeconomics and reality", *Econometrica*, **48**, 1551-1567.
Taylor, J. (1977): "Conditions for a unique solution in stochastic macroeconomic models rational expectations", *Econometrica*, **45**, 1377-1387.
Whiteman, C. H. (1983): *Linear Rational Expectations Models: A User's Guide*, University of Minnesota Press, Minneapolis.

4. DYNAMIC EXTENSIONS

Among the solution methods described in Sections 2 and 3, some may be extended to treat the case of (univariate or multivariate) models involving various expectations. The martingale differences approach allows for the substitution of any expectation in terms of a realization and a prediction error. Starting from the initial structural model, this method leads to a dynamic equation including observable variables and prediction errors. This equation is then used for completely solving the model. This section will begin with some examples. It will be emphasized that, when some dynamic complications arise, it is necessary to impose some constraints on the successive prediction errors. An illustration will give an intuition idea of the general result concerning the solution of set of any linear univariate rational expectations model. After describing this general result, we will apply it to the search for stationary solutions.

1. Some examples

1.1. A model with various expectations of the current endogenous variable

We here consider an extension of the Muth model. The equation includes various expectations of the current endogenous variable formed at different past dates. For instance, when two such expectations are included, the model is given by:

$$y_t = a\,E[y_t|I_{t-1}] + b\,E[y_t|I_{t-2}] + u_t. \tag{4.1}$$

A projection method, similar to the one used to solve the Muth model, may be applied [Aoki and Canzoneri (1980), Visco (1981, 1984)]. Since two expectations are to be replaced, we need two projections. Consequently, we take the expectations of both sides of (4.1), firstly conditional on the information set available at time $t-1$, and then conditional on the information set available at time $t-2$. We obtain a two-equation system:

$$\begin{cases} E[y_t|I_{t-1}] = a\,E[y_t|I_{t-1}] + b\,E[y_t|I_{t-2}] + E[\mu_t|I_{t-1}] \\ E[y_t|I_{t-2}] = a\,E[y_t|I_{t-2}] + b\,E[y_t|I_{t-2}] + E[\mu_t|I_{t-2}] \end{cases}.$$

This system determines uniquely the expectations of the endogenous variable as functions of the expectations of the exogenous variables. Indeed we have:

$$\begin{cases} E[y_t|I_{t-1}] = \dfrac{b}{1-a}\,\dfrac{1}{1-a-b}\,E[u_t|I_{t-2}] + \dfrac{1}{1-a}\,E[u_t|I_{t-1}] \\ E[y_t|I_{t-2}] = \dfrac{1}{1-a-b}\,E[u_t|I_{t-2}]. \end{cases}$$

It follows that model (4.1), like the Muth model, has a unique solution. Explicitly this solution is written as

$$y_t = \frac{b}{(1-a)(1-a-b)}\,E[u_t|I_{t-2}] + \frac{a}{1-a}\,E[u_t|I_{t-1}] + u_t.$$

Of course, the dynamics of the endogenous process is only known after the evolution of the exogenous process has been specified. Consider for instance, for u, an autoregressive model of order 1:

$$u_t = \rho\,u_{t-1} + \epsilon_t, \quad |\rho| < 1.$$

If the information set I_t is composed of the past and current values of the exogenous process, then:

$$E[u_t|I_{t-1}] = \rho\,u_{t-1},$$

and

$$E[u_t|I_{t-2}] = \rho^2\,u_{t-2}.$$

The solution becomes:
$$y_t = \frac{b\rho^2}{(1-a)(1-a-b)} u_{t-2} + \frac{a\rho}{1-a} u_{t-1} + u_t.$$

In this expression, two effects may be separated: the direct effect of the exogenous dynamics (term u_t) and the effect passing through the expectations (terms in u_{t-1} and u_{t-2}).

1.2. A model with a two-periods-ahead future expectation

The model considered in section 3 is here modified by replacing the one-period-ahead expectation by a two-period-ahead one. It becomes:

$$y_t = a\, E[y_{t+2} | I_t] + u_t. \tag{4.2}$$

To solve this model, the prediction error over two periods is introduced:

$$v_{t,2} = y_t - E[y_t | I_{t-2}].$$

Substituting for the expectation in (4.2) yields:

$$y_t = a(y_{t+2} - v_{t+2,2}) + u_t.$$

As shown in Section 1, any prediction error may be decomposed as a sum of revision (or updating) terms:

$$v_{t,2} = \epsilon_t^0 + \epsilon_{t-1}^1,$$

where:
$$\epsilon_t^0 = y_t - E[y_t | I_{t-1}],$$
$$\epsilon_{t-1}^1 = E[y_t | I_{t-1}] - E[y_t | I_{t-2}].$$

We then obtain:

$$y_t = a(y_{t+2} - \epsilon_{t+2}^0 - \epsilon_{t+1}^1) + u_t,$$

or equivalently:

$$y_t = \frac{1}{a} y_{t-2} - \frac{1}{a} u_{t-2} + \epsilon_t^0 + \epsilon_{t-1}^1, \tag{4.3}$$

where ϵ^0 and ϵ^1 are martingale differences.

Conversely, for any given martingale differences ϵ^0 and ϵ^1 and any process y satisfying the latter equation, we directly obtain the two-periods-ahead prediction by taking the expectation conditional on I_{t-2}:

$$E[y_t | I_{t-2}] = \frac{1}{a} y_{t-2} - \frac{1}{a} u_{t-2} + E[\epsilon_t^0 | I_{t-2}] + E[\epsilon_{t-1}^1 | I_{t-2}]$$

$$= \frac{1}{a} y_{t-2} - \frac{1}{a} u_{t-2}.$$

This equation exactly coincides with the initial rational expectations model.

In summary, all solutions of Model (4.2) are given by Equation (4.3) where ϵ^0 and ϵ^1 are arbitrary martingale differences. Since two such arbitrary processes are required for an exhaustive description of the solution set, we will say that this set has a dimension equal to two (in terms of arbitrary martingale differences).

1.3. A model with one current expectation and one future expectation

In Section 3, we have presented a slightly simplified version of the Taylor (1977) model. Actually, the original model considered by Taylor is a rational expectations macromodel leading to a price equation having the following form:

$$y_t = a\, E[y_{t+1} | I_{t-1}] + b\, E[y_t | I_{t-1}] + u_t. \tag{4.4}$$

This equation includes two expectations simultaneously. Both expectations are formed at time $t-1$, however the first one concerns a future variable y_{t+1} while the second one concerns the current variable y_t.

Let us now introduce the prediction errors over one and two periods and then decompose them with the use of revision terms. We obtain:

$$y_t = a(y_{t+1} - \epsilon_{t+1}^0 - \epsilon_t^1) + b(y_t - \epsilon_t^0) + u_t, \tag{4.5}$$

where ϵ^0 and ϵ^1 are martingale differences. Thus any solution to (4.4) verifies (4.5).

Alternatively, let us consider a solution to (4.5) where ϵ^0 and ϵ^1 are taken as arbitrary martingale differences. We will examine whether these processes may be interpreted as updating terms. For this purpose, we successively compute the expectations of both sides of (4.5) conditional on I_t and I_{t-1}. We have:

$$y_t = a(E[y_{t+1} | I_t] - \epsilon_t^1) + b(y_t - \epsilon_t^0) + u_t, \tag{4.6}$$

$$E[y_t | I_{t-1}] = a E[y_{t+1} | I_{t-1}] + b\, E[y_t | I_{t-1}] + E[u_t | I_{t-1}]. \tag{4.7}$$

Taking side by side the difference between (4.6) and (4.5) yields:
$$0 = a(y_{t+1} - E[y_{t+1}|I_t] - \epsilon_{t+1}^0).$$

Consequently, the martingale difference ϵ^0 is necessarily the one-period-ahead prediction error process.

Let now substract (4.7) from (4.6) to obtain:
$$y_t - E[y_t|I_{t-1}] = a(E[y_{t+1}|I_t] - E[y_{t+1}|I_{t-1}] - \epsilon_t^1)$$
$$+ b(y_t - E[y_t|I_{t-1}] - \epsilon_t^0) + u_t - E[u_t|I_{t-1}].$$

Taking into account the previously established form of ϵ^0, one obtains:
$$\epsilon_t^0 = a(E[y_{t+1}|I_t] - E[y_{t+1}|I_{t-1}] - \epsilon_t^1) + u_t - E[u_t|I_{t-1}].$$

It follows that ϵ^1 can be interpreted as the updating term
$$E[y_{t+1}|I_t] - E[y_{t+1}|I_{t-1}]$$
if and only if ϵ^0 fulfills the relation:
$$\epsilon_t^0 = u_t - E[u_t|I_{t-1}].$$

Thus Equation (4.5) represents a too wide formulation for our problem. It provides solutions to Model (4.4) only if one of the martingale differences is subject to an additional constraint. More precisely, for Model (4.4) the constraint requires the one-period-ahead prediction error on y to coincide with the one-period-ahead prediction error on u. We incorporate this restriction and derive the equation involving observable variables that is equivalent to the model. It is given by:
$$y_t = a[y_{t+1} - (u_{t+1} - E[u_{t+1}|I_t]) - \epsilon_t^1]$$
$$+ b[y_t - (u_t - E[u_t|I_{t-1}])] + u_t,$$
or
$$y_t = \frac{1-b}{a} y_{t-1} + u_t - E[u_t|I_{t-1}] + \frac{b-1}{a} u_{t-1}$$
$$- \frac{b}{a} E[u_{t-1}|I_{t-2}] + \epsilon_t^1, \tag{4.8}$$

where ϵ^1 is an arbitrary martingale difference. In terms of this kind of process, the dimension of the solution set is equal to 1.

1.4. Some remarks

Let us now summarize the insights brought by the preceding examples. The first, and probably most obvious, distinction among models concerns the presence or absence of multiple solutions. In our examples, uniqueness occurs for the first model as well as for the Muth model. In turn, non-uniqueness is characteristic of the last two models and the hyperinflation price equation. In the next subsection, we will analyse the linear rational expectations models in more depth and provide a classification based on the non-uniqueness criterion.

On the other hand, the solution methods used above are different depending on the form of the model. The Muth model and its extension have been solved with the help of a projection technique while the other models have been treated by the martingale difference method. This difference is actually inessential. As will be shown, the martingale difference method applies in all cases. Nevertheless, when a projection technique works, it is often more intuitive and also shorter.

From a more technical point of view, the last two examples show that the key aspect of the martingale difference method lies in the introduction of updating terms. Hence not only prediction errors (as one could think after the reading of Section 3) play a crucial role in the determination of the solution set. Furthermore the updating terms are sometimes subject to constraints. The next subsection will begin with a systematic discussion about the necessary constraints that have to be incorporated in the solution phase of the general model. Since the very simple models do not require such constraints, they hide somewhat the presence of this additional level of complexity. By not taking into account this phenomenon, one would enlarge abusively the solution set. As will be shown, the dimension of this set (in terms of martingale differences) varies according to the number and the type of expectations included in the model.

2. Solutions to the general univariate model

2.1. The model

In the case of a single endogenous variable, the most general linear rational expectations model is given by:

$$y_t = \sum_{k=0}^{K} \sum_{h=1}^{H} a_{kh} E[y_{t+h-k} | I_{t-k}] + \sum_{k=1}^{K} a_{k0} y_{t-k} + u_t. \quad (4.9)$$

The current endogenous variable depends on its lagged values y_{t-1}, ..., y_{t-K}, on the exogenous variable u_t and various expectations. Note that u_t summarizes all non-endogenous terms, either disturbances or exogenous factors.

The expectations may concern future values ($h > k$), current ones ($h = k$) or even past ones ($h < k$). Only expectations formed later than the current period are excluded for obvious reasons.

We have taken the same upper value for both sums involving the index k. This simplifies the technical derivations and does not restrict the presentation. It suffices to impose zero values for coefficients that affect non-desirable terms.

Index h has an important meaning. It represents the horizon of the expectations. We assume here that H is chosen as small as possible (i.e. at least one coefficient a_{kH} is different from zero). Therefore H denotes the maximal horizon of the expectations appearing in model (4.9).

2.2. *Expression of the expectations in terms of realizations*

We outline here in a general way the computations that have been used, case by case, in the examples. Any expectation can be expressed by means of the corresponding realization and updating terms:

$$E[y_{t+h-k}|I_{t-k}] = y_{t+h-k} - \sum_{j=0}^{h-1} \epsilon_{t+h-k-j}^j.$$

We then perform the replacement for each expectation in model (4.9) and obtain:

$$y_t = \sum_{k=0}^{K} \sum_{h=1}^{H} a_{kh}\left(y_{t+h-k} - \sum_{j=0}^{h-1} \epsilon_{t+h-k-j}^j\right) + \sum_{k=1}^{K} a_{k0} y_{t-k} + u_t.$$

In this expression, endogenous variables appear in various terms. We group all of the endogenous variables that have the same time index. For this purpose we introduce a new notation a_i^* that represents the sum of all structural coefficients associated with the endogenous variable y_{t+i}. We thus define:

$$a_i^* = \sum_{\substack{k \in \{0,\ldots,K\} \\ i+k \in \{0,\ldots,H\}}} a_{k,i+k},$$

and the equation becomes:

$$\sum_{i=J_0}^{J_1} a_i^* y_{t+i} = \sum_{k=0}^{K} \sum_{h=1}^{H} a_{kh} \sum_{j=0}^{h-1} \epsilon_{t+h-k-j}^j - u_t. \qquad (4.10)$$

The integers J_0 and J_1 are the extreme values taken by index i.

$$J_0 = \min\ \{i: a_i^* \neq 0\},\ J_1 = \max\ \{i: a_i^* \neq 0\}. \qquad (4.11)$$

Equation (4.10) includes H updating processes $\epsilon^0, \epsilon^1, \ldots \epsilon^{H-1}$. Each of them is a martingale difference (see Section 1). At this stage only replacements have been made. The remainder of this discussion will concern the constraints that can arise among the updating terms.

In other respects, note that the perfect foresight model associated with model (4.9) could be solved along the same lines. In this case however, all the updating terms necessarily vanish. Thus, Equation (4.10) with zero values for all the martingale differences $\epsilon^0, \epsilon^1, \ldots \epsilon^{H-1}$ may be seen as the perfect foresight version of the general model. In this case, only u_t appears on the right-hand-side while the left-hand-side includes the autoregressive terms $\sum_{i=J_0}^{J_1} a_i^* y_{t+i}$. It follows that the autoregressive term in (4.10) may be viewed as a summary of the dynamics of the corresponding perfect foresight model.

2.3. Constraints on the updating terms

It has been shown previously that any solution to the general model satisfies Equation (4.10). In this equation any updating term appears as a distinct martingale difference. Now conversely, we will examine whether any arbitrary choice of martingale differences in (4.10) leads to a solution y of the original model.

As emphasized with the example described in subsection 1.3, the martingale differences may not always be taken arbitrarily. Their interpretation as updating terms generally imposes some constraints on the processes denoted $\epsilon^0, \ldots \epsilon^{H-1}$. These necessary and sufficient constraints are described in the following property [see Broze, Gouriéroux and Szafarz (1985) for a proof].

Property (4.12):

a) The solutions to Equation (4.10) satisfy the rational expectations model (4.9) if the martingale differences fulfill the following constraints

$$\epsilon_t^i = \sum_{k=0}^{i} \sum_{h=0}^{H} a_{kh} \epsilon_t^{h-k+i} + E[u_{t+i}|I_t] + E[u_{t+i}|I_{t-i}],$$

$i = 0, \ldots H - J_1 - 1$, for $H > J_1$.

b) If $H = J_1$, the martingale differences may be chosen arbitrarily. In particular the Cagan model and the example of subsection 1.2 correspond to cases where $H = J_1$ and therefore do not include constraints.

2.4. Some consequences

a) Property (4.12) provides the "dimension" of the solution set in terms of martingale differences. Indeed, from the start, H martingale differences are introduced. Among them, $H - J_1$ linear constraints must be imposed. After having solved this system, J_1 arbitrary martingale differences remain.

b) We have already mentioned that multiplicity of solutions in models involving future rational expectations has two components. The first component results from the internal dynamics of the corresponding perfect foresight model, i.e. the fact that y_t generally depends on its lagged values. More precisely, it is clear from (4.10) that lagged endogenous terms enter the reduced form when $J_1 \neq J_0$. However, this first type of non-uniqueness may be avoided by imposing initial conditions on the endogenous process. The second component of the multiplicity is due to the presence of martingale differences that may be chosen arbitrarily. This occurs when $J_1 > 0$. This second component cannot be avoided with initial conditions. The class of models that do not lead to such multiplicity is characterized by the next property.

Property (4.13): The rational expectations models for which any solution may be characterized by a finite number of initial values corresponds to the case $J_1 = 0$.

These models include no future expectations. Their general formulation is:

$$y_t = \sum_{k=0}^{K} \sum_{h=1}^{k} a_{kh} E[y_{t+h-k} | I_{t-k}] + \sum_{k=1}^{K} a_{k0} y_{t-k} + u_t.$$

Property (4.14): The rational expectations models which admit a unique solution are characterized by: $J_0 = J_1 = 0$.

Formally the unique solution models are given by:

$$y_t = \sum_{k=1}^{K} a_{kk} E[y_t | I_{t-k}] + u_t.$$

They only include current expectations and can be easily solved by using a recursive projection technique as illustrated in example 1.2.

c) One might examine under what condition a backward solution exists. Such a solution corresponds to the case where the rational expectations are taken to be perfect. In other words, a backward solution is a solution for which the martingale differences $\epsilon^0, \ldots \epsilon^{H-1}$ are all identically zero. Since constraints are imposed on these processes, the question one has to answer is whether zero values for the martingale differences are compatible with the constraints arising among the updating terms. Considering the system described by property (4.12), it appears that if $H > J_1$ the previous compatibility implies the condition $E[u_{t+i} | I_t] = E[u_{t+i} | I_{t-1}]$ for $i = 0, \ldots H-1$. This condition imposes a predetermined exogenous process, i.e. a much stronger restriction. Therefore a backward solution can be found only when $H = J_1$.

2.5. Some applications

We have summarized in Table III the reduced forms of various rational expectations models. For clarity, we have also given the values of the indexes H, K and J_1.

In Table III, all constraints have been incorporated, hence any updating process ϵ^i that appears should be interpreted as an arbitrary martingale difference.

The models considered here as examples have been chosen in order to recall the main cases used in practical applications and to illustrate the most relevant technical complications that may arise in reducing the models. In fact, the indexes H and K refer to the model itself, while J_1 gives the dimension of the multiplicity (in terms of martingale differences). For instance, one can compare models having the same values for H and K and observe that some but not all have different values for J_1. Two such situations are present in Table III. For $H = 1$ and $K = 1$, the Muth model (line 1) and a future expectations model including a lagged endogenous variable (line 4) are distinct with respect to the multiplicity. The first has a unique solution while the second leads to a reduced form with one arbitrary martingale difference. On

TABLE III

Model	H	K	J_1	Reduced form
$y_t = aE[y_t\|I_{t-1}] + u_t$ (Muth)	1	1	0	$y_t = \dfrac{a}{1-a} E[u_t\|I_{t-1}] + u_t$
$y_t = aE[y_{t+1}\|I_t] + u_t$ (Cagan)	1	0	1	$y_t = \dfrac{1}{a} y_{t-1} - \dfrac{1}{a} u_{t-1} + \epsilon_t^0$
$y_t = aE[y_{t+1}\|I_{t-1}] + u_t$	2	1	1	$y_t = \dfrac{1}{a} y_{t-1} - \dfrac{1}{a} u_{t-1} + u_t - E[u_t\|I_{t-1}] + \epsilon_{t-1}^1$
$y_t = aE[y_{t+1}\|I_t] + by_{t-1} + u_t$	1	1	1	$y_t = \dfrac{1}{a} y_{t-1} - \dfrac{1}{b} y_{t-2} + \dfrac{1}{a} u_{t-1} + \epsilon_t^0$
$y_t = aE[y_{t+1}\|I_{t-1}]$ $+ bE[y_t\|I_{t-1}] + u_t$ (Taylor)	2	1	1	$y_t = \dfrac{1+b}{a} y_{t-1} + u_t - E[u_t\|I_{t-1}] + \dfrac{b-1}{a} u_{t-1}$ $- \dfrac{b}{a} E[u_{t-1}\|I_{t-2}] + \epsilon_{t-1}^1$
$y_t = aE[y_{t+2}\|I_t] + u_t$	2	0	2	$y_t = \dfrac{1}{a} y_{t-2} - \dfrac{1}{a} u_{t-2} + \epsilon_t^0 + \epsilon_{t-1}^1$
$y_t = aE[y_{t+2}\|I_t] + bE[y_{t+1}\|I_t]$ $+ u_t$	2	0	2	$y_t = -\dfrac{b}{a} y_{t-1} + \dfrac{1}{a} y_{t-2} - \dfrac{1}{a} u_{t-2} + \epsilon_t^0$ $- \dfrac{b}{a} \epsilon_{t-1}^0 + \epsilon_{t-1}^1$
$y_t = \displaystyle\sum_{h=1}^{H} a_h E[y_{t+h}\|I_t] + u_t$	H	0	H	$y_t = -\dfrac{1}{a_H} \displaystyle\sum_{h=1}^{H-1} a_{H-h} y_{t-h} + \dfrac{1}{a_H} y_{t-H}$ $+ \displaystyle\sum_{h=1}^{H} a_h \sum_{j=0}^{h-1} \epsilon_{t+h-j-H}^j - \dfrac{1}{a_H} u_{t-H}$

the other hand, for $H = 2$ and $K = 1$, the third and fifth models both lead to $J_1 = 1$. Thus even for fixed values of H, K and J_1, one may obtain various types of models.

Finally note that the choice of the time index for the information set appearing in the model influences the reduced form. Compare for instance the Cagan model (line 2) with the modified version where I_t has been replaced by I_{t-1} (line 3). While both models have a reduced form involving one martingale difference, it is obvious that the endogenous variable has different evolutions (see the reduced forms). The main reason for this is the introduction in the second model of two updating terms (with one constraint). Therefore prediction errors on u_t

appear explicitly and generally this model does not admit a backward solution (because $J_1 < H$).

3. Linear solutions

3.1. The general form of the linear solutions
We here assume that the exogenous process has a moving-average representation (possibly non-stationary):

$$u_t = \Theta(L)\tilde{\epsilon}_t,$$

where $\tilde{\epsilon}_t = \begin{cases} \epsilon_t, & \text{if } t \geq 0 \\ 0, & \text{otherwise} \end{cases}$, with (ϵ_t) being a white noise process.

We are interested in linear solutions to the general model, i.e. in solutions to (4.9) that admit a moving-average formulation of the same type:

$$y_t = A(L)\tilde{\epsilon}_t = a_0 \epsilon_t + a_1 \epsilon_{t-1} + \ldots + a_t \epsilon_0.$$

Obviously, for these solutions, the updating terms must be proportional to the innovation of the exogenous process:

$$\epsilon_t^j = a_j \epsilon_t, \forall j. \tag{4.15}$$

Conversely, to obtain all the linear solutions, it suffices to select among the martingale differences having the previous form the ones that satisfy the constraints.

3.2. (Asymptotic) stationarity of the linear solutions
We now impose (asymptotic) stationarity of the exogenous process and examine whether some of the linear solutions are also (asymptotically) stationary, i.e. are such that $\sum_{j=0}^{\infty} a_j^2 < \infty$.

As shown in subsection 2, the constraints linking the martingale differences allow all of them to be expressed in terms of the J_1 last differences $\epsilon^{H-J_1}, \ldots \epsilon^{H-1}$ that are not restricted. We may then substitute for the first martingale differences in Equation (4.10) and obtain a relation of the following type:

$$\sum_{i=J_0}^{J_1} a_i^* y_{t+i} = \sum_{j=H-J_1}^{H-1} \sum_{k=k_j}^{K_j} c_{jk} \epsilon_{t+J_1-k}^j + g_{t+J_1}(u)$$

where $g_t(u)$ is a mapping of the process u that depends linearly on past and current values of u and of its expectations. As long as a linear stationary representation has been chosen for the exogenous process, the mapping $g_t(u)$ has the same form:

$$g_t(u) = \Omega(L)\epsilon_t$$

Thus the linear solutions are parameterized by the coefficients denoted a_j, $j = H - J_1, \ldots, H - 1$ and are given by:

$$\sum_{i=J_0}^{J_1} a_i^* y_{t+i} = \sum_{j=H-J_1}^{H-1} \left(\sum_{k=k_j}^{K_j} c_{jk} a_j L^{k-J_1} \right) \tilde{\epsilon}_t + \Omega(L)\tilde{\epsilon}_{t+J_1}$$

or equivalently:

$$\left(\sum_{i=0}^{J_1-J_0} a_{J_1-i}^* L^i \right) y_t = \left(\sum_{j=H-J_1}^{H-1} \sum_{k=k_j}^{K_j} c_{jk} a_j L^k + \Omega(L) \right) \tilde{\epsilon}_t \qquad (4.16)$$

Equation (4.16) provides an autoregressive-moving-average form for the linear solutions. Nevertheless, in order to discuss their stationarity, it is necessary to examine the roots of the autoregressive polynomial. More precisely, we must know their position with respect to the unit circle.

Suppose for instance that the autoregressive polynomial has one root, say γ_1, inside the unit circle. It is possible to eliminate this unstable root by imposing that γ_1 is also a root of the moving-average polynomial. This implies the following constraint:

$$\sum_{j=H-J_1}^{H-1} \sum_{k=k_j}^{K_j} c_{jk} a_j \gamma_1^k - \Omega(\gamma_1) = 0.$$

It is thus an additional restriction on the parameters $a_{H-J_1}, \ldots, a_{H-1}$. One may of course proceed in the same way to eliminate every unstable root of the autoregressive polynomial. To each unstable root will correspond a new restriction. This yields the next property.

Property (4.18): Let N be the number of roots of the equation:

$$\sum_{i=0}^{J_1-J_0} a_{J_1-i}^* \gamma^i = 0,$$

that lie inside the unit circle.

- If $J_1 - N > 0$, the general linear stationary solution includes $J_1 - N$ arbitrary scalar parameters;
- If $J_1 = N$, there exists a unique linear stationary solution;
- If $J_1 - N < 0$, no linear stationary solutions exist.

3.3. An example
Let us consider the following model:
$$y_t = a\,E[y_{t+2}|I_t] + b\,E[y_{t+1}|I_t] + \epsilon_t, \quad a \neq 0.$$

From Table III, the general solution to this model is given by:
$$y_t = -\frac{b}{a} y_{t-1} + \frac{1}{a} y_{t-2} - \frac{1}{a} \epsilon_{t-2} + \epsilon_t^0 - \frac{b}{a} \epsilon_{t-1}^0 + \epsilon_{t-1}^1.$$

The linear solutions are deduced from this expression by taking $\epsilon_t^0 = a_0 \epsilon_t$ and $\epsilon_t^1 = a_1 \epsilon_t$. After replacements, we obtain:
$$y_t = -\frac{b}{a} y_{t-1} + \frac{1}{a} y_{t-2} - \frac{1}{a} \epsilon_{t-2} + a_0 \epsilon_t - \frac{b}{a} a_0 \epsilon_{t-1} + a_1 \epsilon_{t-1},$$

or with the use of lag-polynomials:
$$(a + bL - L^2)y_t = (a\,a_0 + (a\,a_1 - b\,a_0)L - L^2)\epsilon_t$$

Various cases are then to be distinguished according to the position of the roots of the autoregressive polynomial $a + b\gamma - \gamma^2$.

i) If both roots lie outside the unit circle, there exists a double infinity of linear stationary solutions that are parameterized by a_0 and a_1.

ii) If only one of these roots lies outside the unit circle, there exists a simple infinity of linear stationary solutions. Letting γ_1 denote the unstable root, the parameters a_0 and a_1 are constrained by the relation:
$$a\,a_0 + (a\,a_1 - b\,a_0)\gamma_1 - \gamma_1^2 = 0.$$

iii) If both roots lie inside (or on) the unit circle, then there exists a unique linear stationary solution. Since $y_t = \epsilon_t$ is clearly a solution to the original model, it necessarily coincides with this particular solution.

In this example it is easy to see that the approach followed here to determine the linear stationary solutions has the advantage of immediately providing their ARMA representation. Indeed, the general expression of the linear solution shows an ARMA (2,2) form. Any explosive root that has to be cancelled implies the reduction by one degree of both the autoregressive and moving-average polynomials. Thus case (ii) corresponds to an infinity of ARMA (1,1) processes, while case (iii) leads to a white noise. The same argument could be put in a more general fashion to discuss the orders of the ARMA solutions of the general model [Evans and Honkapohja (1986), Whiteman (1983), Gouriéroux, Laffont and Monfort (1982)].

References

Aoki, M. and M. Canzoneri (1979): "Reduced forms of rational expectations models", *Quarterly Journal of Economics*, 93, 59-71.
Broze, L., C. Gouriéroux and A. Szafarz (1985): "Solutions of dynamic linear rational expectations models", *Econometric Theory*, 1, 341-368.
D'Autume, A. (1988): "On the solution of linear difference equations with rational expectations", Discussion Paper 134, Laboratoire d'Economie Politique, Ecole Normale Supérieure, Paris.
Evans, G. (1985): "The algebra of ARMA processes and the structure of ARMA solutions to a general linear model with rational expectations", INMMS technical report 476, Standford University.
Evans, G. (1986): "Selection criterion for models with non-uniqueness", *Journal of Monetary Economics*, 18, 147-157.
Evans, G. and S. Honkapohja (1986): "A complete characterization of ARMA solutions to linear rational expectations models", *Review of Economic Studies*, 53, 227-239.
Fair, R. and J. Taylor (1983): "Solution and maximum likelihood estimation of dynamic non-linear expectations models", *Econometrica*, 51, 1169-1184.
Gouriéroux, C., J. J. Laffont and A. Monfort (1982): "Rational expectations in linear models: Analysis of solutions", *Econometrica*, 50, 409-425.
McCafferty, S. and R. Driskill (1980): "Problems of existence and uniqueness in nonlinear rational expectations models", *Econometrica*, 48, 1313-1317.
Sargan, J. D. (1984): "Alternative models for rational expectations in some simple irregular cases", Discussion Paper, London School of Economics.
Taylor, J. (1977): "Conditions for a unique solution in stochastic macroeconomic models with rational expectations", *Econometrica*, 45, 1377-1387.
Visco, I. (1981): "On the derivation of reduced forms of rational expectations models", *European Economic review*, 16, 355-365.
Visco, I. (1984): "On linear models with rational expectations: An addendum", *European Economic review*, 24, 113-115.
Whiteman, C. (1983): *Linear Rational Expectations Models: A User's Guide*, Minneapolis, University of Minnesota Press.

5. MULTIVARIATE MODELS

1. Dynamic macroeconometric models

Simulations of economic policies are generally performed using large-scale computerized macroeconomic models. Among the variables appearing in the model, some (the *controls*) are selected and their values are modified. Then the effects of these shocks on the other variables are evaluated. These effects depend on the amplitude of the initial shocks, on the lag between the date of the shock and the time index of the variable of interest and, of course, on the dynamic specification of the model.

These macroeconomic models are generally simultaneous equation models with a large number of equations and variables. The dynamics is often introduced by means of lagged endogenous and/or exogenous variables. As an example of such a model, we give below the main equations of a core model summarizing the large-scale French model METRIC.

The variables are shown in Table IV:

TABLE IV

Endogenous variables		*Exogenous variables*	
Production:	Q	Autonomous demand government	
Imports:	M	and foreign demand:	$\overline{A}$
Employment:	N	Population size:	$\overline{N}$
Investment:	I	Foreign prices index:	pe
Capital stock:	K		
Wages:	W		
Domestic price index:	P		
Unemployment rate:	Un		
Production capacity:	Q		
Degree of production capacity utilization:	Uc		

The model contains 10 equations. The first one is the equilibrium condition on the goods market. Equation (2) is the imports equation: the elasticity of demand is equal to $1 + e_4$ in the short run and the price elasticity is constant and equals e_2. In Equation (3) the labor productivity increases at a constant rate and the factors of production are complements. In the investment function (4) the effect of profit and an accelerator phenomenon are simultaneously introduced. The usual Phillips curve given by Equation (5) and Relation (6) describes price changes as a function of wages and of a positive effect of excess demand on the goods market. The other equations have clear interpretations.

Equilibrium equation
(1) $Q_t = c Q_t + I_t - M_t + \overline{A}_t;$

Imports
(2) $M_t = \tilde{M}_0 Q_t (P_t/P_t^e)^{c_2} Uc_t^{e_2};$

Employment
(3) $N_t = \overline{W}_0 \exp(-at) Q_t;$

Investment
(4) $I_t = \nu_2(Q_t - Q_{t-1}) + \theta\left(Q_t - \dfrac{W_t N_t}{P_t}\right);$

Wages
(5) $\text{Log } W_t - \text{Log } W_{t-1} = g_1(\text{Log } P_{t+1} - \text{Log } P_{t-1}) + g_2 Un_t + g_3, \ g_2 < 0;$

Prices
(6) $\text{Log } P_t - \text{Log } P_{t-1} = f_1 Uc_t + f_2\left(\text{Log } \dfrac{W_t N_t}{Q_t} - \text{Log } \dfrac{W_{t-1} N_{t-1}}{Q_{t-1}}\right) + f_3;$

Unemployment rate
(7) $Un_t = 1 - N_t/\overline{N}_t;$

Capital
(8) $K_t - K_{t-1} = I_t;$

Production capacity
(9) $\overline{Q}_t = \nu_1 K_t;$

Degree of production capacity utilization
(10) $Uc_t = Q_t/\overline{Q}_t.$

In such a model, the dynamics is often introduced in a quasi-automatic way in order to have the expected distinction between short run and long run, to obtain a good adequation of the model with the available series and to derive multipliers with natural interpretations. In a second step, it might be useful to have a more precise dynamic specification and in particular to build models distinguishing, for instance, the dynamics associated with expectations from the dynamics associated with growth or adjustment.

In the previous model, expectations might be introduced in several equations. For instance, investment might depend on the expected increase in production, the wage increase might depend on expected inflation, . . . If expectations are introduced in the model, we obtain a multivariate model in which each endogenous variable is expressed as a function of some other endogenous variables, of some expectations, of lagged exogenous and endogenous variables. Therefore, it seems important to extend the study of the previous sections to the case of multivariate models with rational expectations. This problem has essentially been considered in the linear case [see e.g. Wallis (1980), Pesaran (1981, 1987), Wegge (1984), Kollintzas (1985), Broze, Gouriéroux and Szafarz (1989)]. The one-dimensional solution methods can only be generalized in a simple way if some invertibility restrictions are imposed on the structural coefficient matrices. In practice, this is often not the case. If we examine for instance the core model previously described, we see that a number of variables do not appear in each equation. This implies that several structural coefficients are implicitly constrained to be equal to zero and this may introduce some partial recursivities into the system.

In subsection 2, we first consider the straightforward extension of Cagan's model, i.e. of the model with future expectations. In the simple case, it is possible to understand why the univariate results have to be modified in the presence of recursivity.

In subsection 3, we give the general form of a multivariate linear model with rational expectations and we discuss the possibility of writing an equivalent more tractable form. The principle is the analog of the state space representation of linear time series. This canonical representation is then used to describe a general solution method for rational expectations models.

The results are applied in subsection 5 to non-stationary solutions. In particular, we study the case of cointegrated series and establish a representation theorem, giving an equivalent error correction form of the model in the presence of rational expectations.

2. A simple case

A multivariate model that is easy to handle is the straightforward extension of Cagan's model studied in Section 3. The endogenous vector Y_t with n components is expressed as a linear function of the future expectations $E[Y_{t+1}|I_t]$ and of an additional term U_t (with n components) summarizing all exogenous and disturbance effects. This model may be written:

$$Y_t = \pi E[Y_{t+1}|I_t] + U_t, \qquad (5.1)$$

where the matrix π of structural coefficients is n × n and the information set contains past and current values of the various components of Y.

Relation (5.1) may be considered as a simultaneous equation model. Each component $y_t^{(j)}$ of the endogenous vector Y depends on the expectations $E[y_{t+1}^{(i)}|I_t]$, i = 1, ..., n, of all the other components and generally simultaneity occurs since the expectations are held at the present date t.

As an illustration, we can describe explicitly system (5.1) in the two-dimensional case. We obtain:

$$\begin{cases} y_t^{(1)} = \pi_{11} E[y_{t+1}^{(1)}|I_t] + \pi_{12} E[y_{t+1}^{(2)}|I_t] + u_t^{(1)} \\ y_t^{(2)} = \pi_{21} E[y_{t+1}^{(1)}|I_t] + \pi_{22} E[y_{t+1}^{(2)}|I_t] + u_t^{(2)} \end{cases}.$$

Such a system is more or less easy to solve depending on the values of the structural coefficients. Let us for instance assume that $\pi_{11} = \pi_{12} = \pi_{22} = 0$. This condition implies that the matrix π is strictly lower triangular and also nilpotent. In this recursive case, we obtain from the first equation:

$$y_t^{(1)} = u_t^{(1)}.$$

Then it is possible to deduce the expectation: $E[y_{t+1}^{(1)}|I_t] = E[\mu_{t+1}^{(1)}|I_t]$, and, replacing in the second equation, the explicit expression for $y_t^{(2)}$:

$$y_t^{(2)} = \pi_{21} E[\mu_{t+1}^{(1)}|I_t] + u_t^{(2)}.$$

Therefore, it seems natural in solving System (5.1) to take into account the possible block recursivities.

2.1. *The case without recursivities*

The endogenous variables are all simultaneously defined when the structural matrix π is nonsingular. In this case, the solution method based on the prediction error (see Section 3) may be applied. It leads to the following reduced form:

$$Y_t = \pi^{-1} Y_{t-1} - \pi^{-1} U_{t-1} + \epsilon_t,$$

where (ϵ_t) is a n-dimensional vector with arbitrary martingale difference components.

2.2. *The special case of a nilpotent structural matrix*

The assumption that π is invertible is quite strong. In many cases, π has a large number of zero elements. Often only few expectations are taken into account, even when the model involves many variables. Technically, if π is singular, new difficulties emerge. Consider, for instance, the case where π is a nilpotent matrix of index 2 ($\pi^2 = 0$). In this case, a forward-looking approach leads to the *unique solution* of the model:

$$\begin{aligned} Y_t &= \pi\, E[Y_{t+1}|I_t] + U_t \\ &= \pi\, E[(\pi\, E[Y_{t+2}|I_{t+1}] + U_{t+1})|I_t] + U_t \\ &= \pi^2 E[Y_{t+2}|I_t] + \pi\, E[U_{t+1}|I_t] + U_t \\ &= \pi\, E[U_{t+1}|I_t] + U_t. \end{aligned}$$

2.3. The general case

So we have shown that two extreme situations are possible: A n-dimensional solution set on the one hand, a unique solution on the other hand. Actually all the intermediate cases may occur. To obtain a reduced form valid for any matrix π, we may proceed on the following way. We first isolate a submodel of (5.1) in which a nonsingular matrix multiplies the expectation vector. Let Q be an invertible matrix such that $Q\pi Q^{-1}$ is the Jordan form of π:

$$Q\pi Q^{-1} = \begin{bmatrix} P & 0 \\ 0 & N \end{bmatrix},$$

where N is the block associated with the zero eigenvalue. If K_2 denotes the number of zero eigenvalues of π, N is a K_2-square nilpotent matrix and P is a $K_1 = (n - K_2)$-square invertible matrix. Let us then define:

$$Y_t^* = QY_t = \begin{bmatrix} y_t^{*1} \\ y_t^{*2} \end{bmatrix}, \quad U_t^* = QU_t = \begin{bmatrix} u_t^{*1} \\ u_t^{*2} \end{bmatrix},$$

where y^{*1} and u^{*1} are K_1-dimensional.

Using this transformation, model (5.1) may be written as:

$$\left.\begin{aligned} y_t^{*1} &= P\, E[y_{t+1}^{*1}|I_t] + u_t^{*1}, \\ y_t^{*2} &= P\, E[y_{t+1}^{*2}|I_t] + u_t^{*2} \end{aligned}\right\} \qquad (5.2)$$

In this canonical form, the two blocks are totally separated. Each group of variables cannot be influenced by expectations of variables in the other group.

The reduction of the first group of equations is straightforward since P is invertible and the solution is obtained as in subsection 2.2. In the second group of equations, there is a nilpotent matrix N: $N^{K_2} = 0$. A forward-looking approach gives a unique solution:

$$y_t^{*2} = N\,E[y_{t+1}^{*2}|I_t] + u_t^{*2}$$
$$= N^2\,E[y_{t+2}^{*2}|I_t] + N\,E[u_{t+1}^{*2}|I_t] + u_t^{*2}$$
$$\vdots$$
$$= N^{K_2}\,E[y_{t+K_2}^{*2}|I_t] + N^{K_2-1}\,E[u_{t+K_2-1}^{*2}|I_t] + \ldots + u_t^{*2}$$
$$= \sum_{k=0}^{K_2-1} N^k\,E[u_{t+k}^{*2}|I_t].$$

The next property summarizes the results. It generalizes the method proposed by Pesaran (1981) when π has an equivalent diagonal form.

Property (5.3): The solutions of model (5.1) are given by:
$$Y_t = Q^{-1}\,Y_t^*,$$
where Y^* verifies:
$$\begin{cases} y_t^{*1} = P^{-1}\,y_{t-1}^{*1} - P^{-1}\,u_{t-1}^{*1} + \epsilon_t^{*1} \\ y_t^{*2} = \sum_{k=0}^{K_2-1} N^k\,E[u_{t+k}^{*2}|I_t], \end{cases}$$

and ϵ^{*1} is a vector with K_1 arbitrary martingale difference components.

The two extreme cases mentioned at the beginning may be restated according to the general case. First, when π is nonsingular ($K_1 = n$), n arbitrary martingale differences enter the general solution. Secondly, when π is nilpotent ($K_1 = 0$), we have necessarily $\pi^n = 0$ and the solution is unique:

$$Y_t = \sum_{k=0}^{n-1} \pi^k\,E[U_{t+k}|I_t].$$

In particular, if the model is globally recursive, it is possible after a permutation of variables to have for π a strictly lower triangular matrix. In this case, the system may be written as:

$$y_t^{(1)} = u_t^{(1)}$$
$$y_t^{(2)} = \pi_{21}\,E[y_{t+1}^{(1)}|I_t] + u_t^{(2)}$$
$$y_t^{(3)} = \pi_{31}\,E[y_{t+1}^{(1)}|I_t] + \pi_{32}\,E[y_{t+1}^{(2)}|I_t] + u_t^{(3)}$$
$$\vdots$$

and the unique solution may be directly computed by recursive substitutions.

$$y_t^{(1)} = u_t^{(1)}$$
$$y_t^{(2)} = \pi_{21} E[u_{t+1}^{(1)} | I_t] + u_t^{(2)}$$
$$\vdots$$

3. The general model

3.1. Canonical forms

The most general form of a linear simultaneous equations model with rational expectations is the following:

$$\sum_{k=0}^{K} \sum_{h=0}^{H} A_{kh} E[Y_{t+h-k} | I_{t-k}] = U_t, \qquad (5.4)$$

where A_{kh}, $k=0,\ldots,K$, $h=0,\ldots,H$ are $n \times n$ matrices. For a zero horizon ($h=0$), expectations are equal to the actual variables:

$$E[Y_{t-k} | I_{t-k}] = Y_{t-k}, \quad \forall k.$$

Consequently the corresponding terms in (5.4) give the current endogenous variables for $h = k = 0$ and the lagged endogenous variables for $h = 0$ and $k \geq 1$. The usual restriction that A_{00} is regular ensures that the model defines without ambiguity the current terms as functions of lagged values, expectations and disturbances.

In order to determine *canonical forms* of model (5.4) including for instance less distinct expectation terms, we may introduce a "state vector" which summarizes these expectations. Let us define the following vector composed of all expectations held at time t appearing in the model:

$$Z_t = \begin{bmatrix} Y_t \\ E[Y_{t+1} | I_t] \\ \vdots \\ E[Y_{t+H} | I_t] \end{bmatrix}. \qquad (5.5)$$

The size of Z_t is $N = n(H+1)$. With the use of (5.5), model (5.4) may be rewritten equivalently as:

$$\begin{bmatrix} A_{00} & A_{01} & \ldots & A_{0H} \\ 0 & \mathrm{Id} & \ldots & 0 \\ \ldots & \ldots & \ldots & \ldots \\ 0 & \ldots & \ldots & \mathrm{Id} \end{bmatrix} Z_t + \sum_{k=1}^{K} \begin{bmatrix} A_{k0} & A_{k1} & \ldots & A_{kH} \\ & & 0 & \end{bmatrix} Z_{t-k} \quad (5.6)$$

$$+ \begin{bmatrix} 0 & 0 & \ldots & 0 \\ -\mathrm{Id} & 0 & \ldots & 0 \\ 0 & \ldots & -\mathrm{Id} & 0 \end{bmatrix} E[Z_{t+1}|I_t] = \begin{bmatrix} U_t \\ 0 \\ \ldots \\ 0 \end{bmatrix},$$

or with obvious notations:

$$\Gamma_0 Z_t + \Gamma_1 Z_{t-1} + \ldots + \Gamma_K Z_{t-K} + \Gamma_{-1} E[Z_{t+1}|I_t] = V_t. \quad (5.7)$$

This introduction of the state-vector Z thus leads to an equivalent form of the initial model that only includes a one-period-ahead expectation term. In other words, we have reduced the maximum horizon of the model from H to 1. Of course, this is compensated by an increase in the size of the system. Finally we can note that, in the canonical form, coefficient Γ_0 is still a regular matrix.

Property (5.8): Any linear rational expectations model may be written in a canonical form including lagged terms and only a one-period-ahead expectation term.

The previous reduction is specific to rational expectations models. We may now pursue this reduction in the usual way by diminishing the number of lags in the model. To this end, let us introduce a second state-vector denoted by X having the size $n(H+1)K$:

$$X_t = \begin{bmatrix} Z_t \\ Z_{t-1} \\ \ldots \\ Z_{t-K+1} \end{bmatrix} \quad (5.9)$$

From (5.7), we then obtain:

$$\begin{bmatrix} \Gamma_0 & \Gamma_1 & \ldots & \Gamma_{K-1} \\ 0 & \mathrm{Id} & \ldots & 0 \\ \ldots & \ldots & \ldots & \ldots \\ 0 & 0 & \ldots & \mathrm{Id} \end{bmatrix} X_t + \begin{bmatrix} 0 & 0 & \ldots & 0 & \Gamma_K \\ -\mathrm{Id} & 0 & \ldots & \ldots & 0 \\ \ldots & \ldots & \ldots & \ldots & \ldots \\ 0 & \ldots & & -\mathrm{Id} & 0 \end{bmatrix} X_{t-1}$$

$$+ \begin{bmatrix} \Gamma_{-1} & 0 & \ldots & 0 \\ & 0 & & \end{bmatrix} E[X_{t+1}|I_t] = \begin{bmatrix} V_t \\ 0 \\ \ldots \\ 0 \end{bmatrix}. \quad (5.10)$$

Again obvious notations are used to rewrite (5.10) as:

$$\Lambda_0 X_t + \Lambda_1 X_{t-1} + \Lambda_{-1} E[X_{t+1}|I_t] = W_t.$$

In this expression only *one lagged endogenous variable and one rational expectations* are still present. Also, the matrix Λ_0 that multiplies the current endogenous variable is invertible.

Property (5.11): Any linear rational expectations model may be written in a canonical form including only one lagged term and only a one-period-ahead expectation term.

To illustrate the determination of canonical forms, let us consider an example. In order to clarify the derivations, we start from a univariate model:

$$y_t = a_{10} y_{t-1} + a_{20} y_{t-2} + a_{01} E[y_{t+1}|I_t] + a_{02} E[y_{t+2}|I_t] \\ + a_{21} E[y_{t-1}|I_{t-2}] + a_{12} E[y_{t+1}|I_{t+1}] + u_t. \quad (5.12)$$

For this model, the maximum horizon H is equal to 2 and the maximum lag K is also equal to 2. The first state vector Z is thus given by:

$$Z_t = \begin{bmatrix} y_t \\ E[y_{t+1}|I_t] \\ E[y_{t+2}|I_t] \end{bmatrix},$$

and the model may be put in the following form

$$\begin{bmatrix} -1 & a_{01} & a_{02} \\ 0 & 1 & 0 \\ 0 & 0 & 1 \end{bmatrix} Z_t + \begin{bmatrix} a_{10} & 0 & a_{12} \\ 0 & 0 & 0 \\ 0 & 0 & 0 \end{bmatrix} Z_{t-1}$$
$$+ \begin{bmatrix} a_{20} & a_{21} & 0 \\ 0 & 0 & 0 \\ 0 & 0 & 0 \end{bmatrix} Z_{t-2} + \begin{bmatrix} 0 & 0 & 0 \\ -1 & 0 & 0 \\ 0 & -1 & 0 \end{bmatrix} E[Z_{t+1}|I_t] = \begin{bmatrix} u_t \\ 0 \\ 0 \end{bmatrix}.$$

Let us now define the second state-vector X by:

$$X_t = \begin{bmatrix} Z_t \\ Z_{t-1} \end{bmatrix}.$$

This vector has 6 scalar components and leads to the system:

$$\begin{bmatrix} -1 & a_{01} & a_{02} & a_{10} & 0 & a_{12} \\ 0 & 1 & 0 & 0 & 0 & 0 \\ 0 & 0 & 1 & 0 & 0 & 0 \\ 0 & 0 & 0 & 1 & 0 & 0 \\ 0 & 0 & 0 & 0 & 1 & 0 \\ 0 & 0 & 0 & 0 & 0 & 1 \end{bmatrix} X_t + \begin{bmatrix} 0 & 0 & 0 & a_{20} & a_{21} & 0 \\ 0 & 0 & 0 & 0 & 0 & 0 \\ 0 & 0 & 0 & 0 & 0 & 0 \\ -1 & 0 & 0 & 0 & 0 & 0 \\ 0 & -1 & 0 & 0 & 0 & 0 \\ 0 & 0 & -1 & 0 & 0 & 0 \end{bmatrix} X_{t-1}$$

$$+ \begin{bmatrix} 0 & 0 & 0 & 0 & 0 & 0 \\ -1 & 0 & 0 & 0 & 0 & 0 \\ 0 & -1 & 0 & 0 & 0 & 0 \\ 0 & 0 & 0 & 0 & 0 & 0 \\ 0 & 0 & 0 & 0 & 0 & 0 \\ 0 & 0 & 0 & 0 & 0 & 0 \end{bmatrix} E[X_{t+1} | I_t] = \begin{bmatrix} u_t \\ 0 \\ 0 \\ 0 \\ 0 \\ 0 \end{bmatrix}.$$

This canonical form of the initial model only includes two scalar one-period-ahead expectation terms taking into account the coefficients appearing in the matrices. Of course, the counterpart of the simplification in the structure of the system lies in its dimension. However, numerous zero-restrictions and normalization restrictions have been introduced on the elements of the coefficients matrices.

3.2. Reduction of the canonical form

It is obviously equivalent to determine the endogenous processes verifying either the initial model (5.4) or one of its canonical forms, (5.7) or (5.10). In this subsection we will develop a reduction method for the simplest canonical form, i.e. canonical form (5.10). The next subsection will go back to the original model and apply a direct method. We thus propose two different (and theoretically equivalent) answers to the problem of solving the initial model.

Let us now focus on system (5.10) which is given by:

$$\Lambda_0 X_t + \Lambda_1 X_{t-1} + \Lambda_{-1} E[X_{t+1} | I_t] = W_t,$$

where Λ_0 is invertible.

We will here use the *adjoint operator method*. This method is carried out in two steps:

i) The first step involves replacement of the expectation in terms of the corresponding realization. Like in the univariate case, we introduce the predictor error process on X denoted by η:

$$\eta_t = X_t - E[X_t | I_{t-1}]. \tag{5.13}$$

Each component of η is a martingale difference. Substituting the expectation in (5.10) yields:

$$\Lambda_0 X_t + \Lambda_1 X_{t-1} + \Lambda_{-1} X_{t+1} = W_t + \Lambda_{-1} \eta_{t+1}. \tag{5.14}$$

By lagging this relation and by using operator notation, we have:

$$(\Lambda_{-1} + \Lambda_0 L + \Lambda_1 L^2) X_t = W_{t-1} + \Lambda_{-1} \eta_t. \tag{5.15}$$

ii) The second step of the reduction introduces the adjoint matrix, denoted by $\Pi(L)$, of the matrix polynomial $\Lambda_{-1} + \Lambda_0 L + \Lambda_1 L^2$. By applying the operator $\Pi(L)$ to both sides of Equation (5.15) and by rewriting the determinant of $\Lambda_{-1} + \Lambda_0 L + \Lambda_1 L^2$ as $L^G \phi(L)$, with $\phi(0) \neq 0$, we obtain:

$$L^G \phi(L) X_t = \Pi(L) \Lambda_{-1} \eta_t + \Pi(L) W_{t-1}$$

$$\Leftrightarrow L^G \phi(L) X_t = L^G \phi(L) \eta_t - \Pi(L)[\Lambda_0 L + \Lambda_1 L^2] \eta_t + \Pi(L) W_{t-1}$$

$$\Leftrightarrow \phi(L)(X_t - \eta_t) = -\Pi(L)[\Lambda_0 L + \Lambda_1 L^2] \eta_{t+G} + \Pi(L) W_{t+G-1}.$$

Since the series $\phi(L)$ only includes positive powers of L and since $X_t - \eta_t$ only depends on the information set I_{t-1}, both sides of the last equation depend only on the information set I_{t-1}. It follows that the prediction error process (η_t) is constrained, not only by the martingale difference restriction, but also by the relation:

$$E[-\Pi(L)[\Lambda_0 L + \Lambda_1 L^2] \eta_{t+G} + \Pi(L) W_{t+G-1} | I_{t-1}] \tag{5.16}$$
$$= -\Pi(L)[\Lambda_0 L + \Lambda_1 L^2] H_{t+G} + \Pi(L) W_{t+G-1}, \forall t.$$

It may be shown [Broze, Gouriéroux and Szafarz (1989)] that both conditions (5.14) and (5.16) and the martingale difference property provide a characterization of the solution set of model (5.7). More precisely, we have the following result.

Property (5.17): All the solutions of the rational expectations model (5.7) are obtained by taking the martingale differences η that fulfill (5.16) and by solving all the associated difference equations systems:

$$\Lambda_0 X_{t-1} + \Lambda_1 X_{t-2} + \Lambda_{-1} X_t = W_{t-1} + \Lambda_{-1} \eta_t.$$

Consequently, for solving a rational expectations system, one needs to solve many difference equation systems. Actually, each of the latter systems is characterized by the process η entering its RHS. There are thus as many systems as there are admissible η's, i.e.

martingale differences fulfilling (5.16). Generally these restrictions still leave an infinite set of possibilities. Therefore, we obtain an infinite set of difference equation systems and subsequently an infinite set of solutions to the rational expectations model.

The dimension of this set may be evaluated by enumerating the independent constraints imposed on the components of the vector η. Let us first write these constraints in an explicit way. We introduce the matrices $D_0, D_1, \ldots D_k, \ldots$ such that:

$$D_0 + D_1 L + \ldots + D_k L^k + \ldots = -\Pi(L)(\Lambda_0 + \Lambda_1 L).$$

The constraints imposed by (5.16) are:

$$E[(D_0 + D_1 L + \ldots + D_k L^k + \ldots)\eta_{t+G-1} + \Pi(L)W_{t+G-1} | I_{t-1}]$$
$$= (D_0 + D_1 L + \ldots + D_k L^k + \ldots)\eta_{t+G-1} + \Pi(L)W_{t+G-1}.$$

Since η_t is not correlated with past variables, we may deduce the following equivalent system of restrictions:

$$\begin{cases} D_0 \eta_{t+G-1} + \Pi(L)W_{t+G-1} - E[\Pi(L)W_{t+G-1} | I_{t+G-2}] = 0 \\ D_1 \eta_{t+G-2} + E[\Pi(L)W_{t+G-1} | I_{t+G-2}] - E[\Pi(L)W_{t+G-1} | I_{t+G-3}] = 0, \\ \ldots \\ D_{G-1} \eta_t + E[\Pi(L)W_{t+G-1} | I_t] - E[\Pi(L)W_{t+G-1} | I_{t-1}] = 0. \end{cases}$$

This system only includes linear constraints on the prediction error η by linking it to predictions of exogenous factors. Since all equations in the system hold for any time t, we may bring together the ones that are associated with the current value η_t. In so doing, we obtain a system in which the LHS is $[D_0', D_1', \ldots, D_{G-1}']' \eta_t$. Consequently, the value taken by this rank obviously depends on the restrictions imposed on the structural parameters of the model.

3.3. Reduction of the general model

In its initial form, the general linear multivariate rational expectations model is given by:

$$\sum_{k=0}^{K} \sum_{h=0}^{H} A_{kh} E[Y_{t+h-k} | I_{t-k}] = U_t, \tag{5.4}$$

where the endogenous vector Y_t has n components.

In the previous subsection, we have solved out the initial model by making use of its canonical form. It is possible to introduce along the same lines a direct solution method. To understand this method, let us first examine the endogenous vector X_t appearing in the canonical form. This vector has $n(H + 1)K$ components and has been defined by:

$$X_t = \begin{bmatrix} Z_t \\ Z_{t-1} \\ \cdots \\ Z_{t-K+1} \end{bmatrix} \text{ with } Z_t = \begin{bmatrix} Y_t \\ E[Y_{t+1}|I_t] \\ \cdots \\ E[Y_{t+H}|I_t] \end{bmatrix}.$$

According to this definition, the vector η_t representing the prediction error on X_t is given by:

$$\eta_t = \begin{bmatrix} Z_t - E[Z_t|I_{t-1}] \\ 0 \\ \cdots \\ 0 \end{bmatrix},$$

with

$$Z_t - E[Z_t|I_{t-1}] = \begin{bmatrix} Y_t - E[Y_t|I_{t-1}] \\ E[Y_{t+1}|I_t] - E[Y_{t+1}|I_{t-1}] \\ \cdots \\ E[Y_{t+H}|I_t] - E[Y_{t+H}|I_{t-1}] \end{bmatrix}.$$

Thus the components of η_t are the updating terms corresponding to the original process Y (the first one being the prediction error over one period):

$$\epsilon_t^0 = Y_t - E[Y_t|I_{t-1}],$$
$$\cdots$$
$$\epsilon_t^h = E[Y_{t+h}|I_t] - E[Y_{t+h}|I_{t-1}], \ h \geq 1.$$

Therefore, in order to solve directly the initial model, it is natural to replace in model (5.4) the expectations in terms of the realizations. For this purpose we use one-period-ahead prediction errors as well as updating terms. Indeed, for $h \geq 1$, we have:

$$E[Y_{t+h-k}|I_{t-k}] = Y_{t+h-k} - \sum_{j=0}^{h-1} \epsilon_{t+h-k-j}^j.$$

After replacement in the initial model, we obtain (with the convention $\sum_{j=0}^{-1} . = 0$):

$$\sum_{k=0}^{K} \sum_{h=0}^{H} A_{kh} \left[Y_{t+h-k} - \sum_{j=0}^{h-1} \epsilon_{t+h-k-j}^{j} \right] = U_t.$$

This form is equivalent to:

$$\tilde{A}(L)Y_{t+H} = \sum_{k=0}^{K} \sum_{h=1}^{H} A_{kh} \sum_{j=0}^{h-1} \epsilon_{t+h-k-j}^{j} + U_t, \qquad (5.18)$$

where: $\tilde{A}(L) = L^H A(L)$ and $A(L) = \sum_{k=0}^{K} \sum_{h=0}^{H} A_{kh} L^{k-h}$.

Following the adjoint operator method, we now introduce the matrix $\tilde{\Pi}(L)$ such that $\tilde{\Pi}(L)\tilde{A}(L) = L^{\tilde{G}} \tilde{\phi}(L) \mathrm{Id}$, with $\tilde{\phi}(0) \neq 0$. Then by multiplying both sides of (5.18) by $\tilde{\Pi}(L)$, we obtain:

$$L^{\tilde{G}} \tilde{\phi}(L) Y_t = \tilde{\Pi}(L) U_{t-H} + \tilde{\Pi}(L) \sum_{k=0}^{K} \sum_{h=1}^{H} A_{kh} \sum_{j=0}^{h-1} \epsilon_{t+h-H-k-j}^{j}.$$

The LHS of this system only depends on the information set $I_{t-\tilde{G}}$. The same must then be true for the RHS. This constraint leads to the following restrictions imposed on the successive updating terms:

$$E \left[\tilde{\Pi}(L) U_{t-H} + \tilde{\Pi}(L) \sum_{k=0}^{K} \sum_{h=1}^{H} A_{kh} \sum_{j=0}^{h-1} \epsilon_{t+h-H-k-j}^{j} \,\Big|\, I_{t-\tilde{G}} \right] \qquad (5.19)$$

$$= \tilde{\Pi}(L) U_{t-H} + \tilde{\Pi}(L) \sum_{k=0}^{K} \sum_{h=1}^{H} A_{kh} \sum_{j=0}^{h-1} \epsilon_{t+h-H-k-j}^{j}.$$

Property (5.20): All the solutions of the rational expectations model (5.4) are obtained by taking the martingale differences $\epsilon^0, \ldots, \epsilon^{H-1}$ (interpreted as updating processes) that fulfill (5.19) and solving all the associated difference equation systems:

$$A(L) Y_t = U_t + \sum_{k=0}^{K} \sum_{h=1}^{H} A_{kh} \sum_{j=0}^{h-1} \epsilon_{t+h-k-j}^{j}.$$

The rank of System (5.19) giving the linear constraints varies according to the structure of the model. Since this rank gives the number of independent constraints imposed on $\epsilon^0, \ldots, \epsilon^{H-1}$ and consequently the degree of multiplicity of the solution set of (5.4), we call the *degree of multiplicity* the number of scalar martingale differences that may be chosen arbitrarily. This number is equal to nH minus the rank of system (5.19). The following result concerning the degree of multiplicity can be derived [Broze, Gouriéroux and Szafarz (1989)].

Property (5.21): If the structural parameters A_{kh}, $k=0, \ldots, K$, $h=0, \ldots, H$, are only subject to exclusion restrictions, the degree of multiplicity is equal to nH − G where n is the size of the vector Y, H is the maximum horizon of the model and G is the number of zero-roots of the characteristic equation det $\tilde{A}(L) = 0$.

Actually it is equivalent to solve directly System (5.4) or to first apply a state-vector transformation and then reduce the simpler canonical form. In both cases, the general solution has the same expression. The difference only lies in the technical steps of the derivation.

3.4. Linear stationary solutions

We now assume that the exogenous process admits an ARMA representation based on the independent white noise:

$$\Phi(L)U_t = \Theta(L)\epsilon_t,$$

where the degrees of the matrix polynomials Φ and Θ are respectively p and q.

Let us search for the solutions to (5.4) admitting a moving-average form based on the same noise ϵ, i.e. the solutions that may be written as:

$$Y_t = \sum_{j=0}^{\infty} C_j \epsilon_{t-j}.$$

For these processes, the successive updating terms are given by:

$$\epsilon_t^j = C_j \epsilon_t.$$

Leaving aside the constraints, we know that any such solution satisfies the following system:

$$A(L)Y_t = U_t + \sum_{k=0}^{K} \sum_{h=1}^{H} A_{kh} \sum_{j=0}^{h-1} \epsilon_{t+h-k-j}^j.$$

Consequently it necessarily satisfies:

$$A(L)Y_t = \Phi^{-1}(L)\Theta(L)\epsilon_t + \sum_{k=0}^{K} \sum_{h=1}^{H} A_{kh} \sum_{j=0}^{h-1} C_j \epsilon_{t+h-k-j},$$

$$\Phi(L)\tilde{A}(L)Y_t = \Theta(L)L^H \epsilon_t + \Phi(L) \sum_{k=0}^{K} \sum_{h=1}^{H} A_{kh} \sum_{j=0}^{h-1} C_j L^{H-h+k+j} \epsilon_t.$$

(5.22)

With reference to this expression, we may compute the orders of the ARMA representation of the process Y.

Property (5.23): If the exogenous process U in (5.4) has an ARMA (p, q) representation $\Phi(L)U_t = \Theta(L)\epsilon_t$, then all the linear stationary solutions of the model have an ARMA representation such that:

i) the autoregressive polynomial is $\Phi(L)\tilde{A}(L)$;

ii) the moving-average polynomial has a degree smaller than or equal to $\text{Max}\{q+H, p+H+K-1\}$;

iii) the parameters C_j may be expressed as functions of the first H parameters $C_0, \ldots C_{H-1}$ and the structural parameters Φ, Θ and A_{kh}.

Actually (iii) allows for taking into account (5.22) as well as the system of constraints (5.19). Note also that property (5.23) does not ensure existence of a linear stationary solution. As we know from Section 4, even in the case of a univariate model, such solutions may not exist.

4. Rational expectations and non-stationary models

Previously we have often considered stationary solutions of rational expectations models. Obviously such an approach makes sense only when the processes of interest may present a stationary evolution. This will be the case of variables expressing growth rates, for instance the inflation rate or exchange rate movements. Other examples are provided by the variables measuring a disequilibrium, such as the rate of unemployment and the excess production capacity, or more generally, by any variable expressed as a deviation from an equilibrium value.

On the other hand, it is sometimes interesting to formulate models that include real variables instead of growth rates. In particular this is important if one is concerned with the study of the growth paths of the economy. In such a case, the model should necessarily lead to non-stationary solutions.

In the first subsection, 4.1, we recall the usual modelling for non-stationary series, and some characteristics of joint series of this kind. Subsequently, we introduce the notion of cointegrated series and the error correction representation of a non-stationary dynamic model.

The second subsection, 4.2, is concerned with a rational expectations model for which the corresponding perfect foresight model admits non-stationary solutions. We show that the linear solutions of the rational expectations model are also non-stationary. Furthermore, these solutions have the same long-term properties as the solutions of the perfect foresight model. Finally we give the error correction form of the rational expectations model.

4.1. Decomposition of an ARIMA series and cointegration

(i) The VAR model The theory of non-stationary series has mostly been developed for series having a polynomial trend. This approach allows the taking into account of exponential growth, after having log-transformed the original series.

Such polynomial series are usually modelled by means of vector-autoregressive (VAR) representations:

$$\Phi(L)Y_t = \epsilon_t, \ t \geq 0; \ Y_t = 0 \text{ for } t < 0. \tag{5.24}$$

The components of the vector Y_t are the observations of the various series at each date. The size of Y_t is equal to the number, n, of variables appearing in the model. The operator $\Phi(L)$ is a lag-polynomial of order p with matrix coefficients, each of them having the size n × n. ϵ denotes a n-dimensional white noise having an invertible covariance matrix. It follows that the components of the noise are not multicollinear.

In expression (5.24), each variable Y_{it} is given in terms of the current values of the other variables, the past values of all the variables and an error term.

From the autoregressive representation, other equivalent formulations may be deduced. For instance, let us introduce the adjoint matrix of $\Phi(L)$ which is denoted by $\Phi^*(L)$. By multiplying both sides of (5.24) by $\Phi^*(L)$, we obtain:

$$\det \Phi(L) Y_t = \Phi^*(L)\epsilon_t, \ t \geq 0. \tag{5.25}$$

This system may be written equation by equation. The ith equation is:

$$\det \Phi(L) Y_{it} = \Phi_i^*(L) \epsilon_t.$$

$$\Leftrightarrow Y_{it} = \frac{\Phi_i^*(L)}{\det \Phi(L)} \tilde{\epsilon}_t, \text{ where } \tilde{\epsilon}_t = \begin{cases} \epsilon_t & \text{if } t \geq 0. \\ 0 & \text{otherwise.} \end{cases}$$

Consequently the ith series has an ARMA form. In order to include some non-stationarity in the series, we assume that the autoregressive part of this ARMA form has a root equal to 1. If the same assumption applies to all the components of Y, then every $(Y_{it}, i=1, \ldots n)$, is a non-stationary process, while every differenciated series $(Y_{it} - Y_{i,t-1})$, $i=1, \ldots n$ is stationary. The original system may then be rewritten as:

$$(1-L)Y_t = H(L)\tilde{\epsilon}_t, \tag{5.26}$$

where the ith row of the operator $H(L)$ is given by:

$$H_i(L) = \frac{\Phi_i^*(L)(1-L)}{\det \Phi(L)}.$$

The elements of this ith row are taken to be such that $H_i(L)$ is not divisible by $(1-L)$. (Otherwise the ARMA representation of the ith series would admit a double unit root for its autoregressive part, this situation being excluded here). The series (Y_{it}), $i=1 \ldots n$ are then said to be first-order integrated.

(ii) Cointegration The previous argument is developed for each component of Y_t. In other words, it is based on a univariate expression of each series Y_{it}, $i=1, \ldots n$. Cointegration is based on a specific multivariate analysis of the whole vector-series Y_t.

Each series Y_{it} is non-stationary with a trend. We may wish to separate the explosive part of Y_t from its stationary part. The following expression provides such a decomposition:

$$Y_t = \frac{H(1)}{1-L} \tilde{\epsilon}_t + \frac{H(L) - H(1)}{1-L} \tilde{\epsilon}_t.$$

In this expression, each $H_i(1)$ is different from zero and the first term is a linear combination of the random walks $1/(1-L) \tilde{\epsilon}_{jt}$, $j=1, \ldots n$. Consequently each $Y_{it}^e = H_i(1)\tilde{\epsilon}_t/(1-L)$ is explosive, in the sense that its variance tends to infinity with t.

On the other hand, $H(L) - H(1)$ is divisible by $1-L$ and the second component $Y_{it}^S = H_i(L) - H_i(1)/(1-L)\, \tilde{\epsilon}_t$ is stationary.

This decomposition into an explosive part and a stationary part is applicable not only to the initial series Y_t, but also to any linear combination of its components. Let $\alpha' Y_t = \sum_{i=1}^{n} \alpha_i Y_{it}$ be such a linear combination. We obtain:

$$\alpha' Y_t = \frac{\alpha' H(1)}{1-L} \tilde{\epsilon}_t + \alpha' \frac{H(L) - H(1)}{1-L} \tilde{\epsilon}_t.$$

As already mentioned, the rows of matrix $H(1)$ are not identically zero. However it is possible that the vector $\alpha' H(1)$ is equal to zero. This could happen when $H(1)$ is a singular matrix. In such a case, there would exist some stationary combinations of series that are all non-stationary. We then say that the series are *cointegrated*. More precisely, Granger (1986) gives the following definitions.

Definition (5.27):

i) The non-stationary series (Y_{it}), $i = 1, \ldots n$, are cointegrated if there exists a non-zero linear combination of the components that is stationary.

ii) When the one-dimensional series are first-order integrated, there is cointegration if and only if matrix $H(1)$ is singular.

iii) A *cointegration vector* is any vector providing a stationary linear cointegration combination. Thus the vectors are defined through the condition: $H(1)'\alpha = 0$.

(iii) The error correction form (Davidson, Hendry, Srba and Yeo (1978)) To each cointegration vector α corresponds a relation of the following kind:

$$\alpha' Y_t = \alpha_1 Y_{1t} + \ldots + \alpha_n Y_{nt} = u_t, \qquad (5.28)$$

where (u_t) denotes a stationary process. Actually, this relation may be decomposed into two relations which respectivelyl concern the explosive components and the stationary components of the series.

For the explosive components, we have a strictly deterministic relation, i.e. a relation that does not include an error term.

$$\alpha_1 Y_{1t}^e + \ldots + \alpha_n Y_{nt}^e = 0.$$

For the residual components, we have then:

$$\alpha_1 Y^s_{it} + \ldots + \alpha_n Y^s_{nt} = u_t.$$

In the literature, Equation (5.28) is often called the *long-term equilibrium relation* (a better term would be: "the relation between dominant components") and u_t is consequently called the *equilibrium error term*.

Usually, the models are built in two steps. First the long-term relations are specified. Then the adjustment factors around the long-term are added. The *error correction representation* of cointegrated series has the advantage of clearly distinguishing these two steps. Indeed this representation is seen to link the equilibrium error terms and the modifications brought to the various economic variables of the model.

More precisely, if r denotes the kernel dimension of the matrix H(1), and if $\Omega = [\alpha_1, \ldots, \alpha_r]$ is a n × r matrix whose row-vectors form a base in the cointegration vector space, then the representation is given by the following result.

Representation Theorem (5.29): [Engle and Granger (1987)].

There exist a n × r matrix Δ and an autoregressive polynomial $\tilde{\Phi}(L)$ such that the original model (5.24) is equivalent to:

$$\Delta \Omega' Y_t + \tilde{\Phi}(L)(Y_t - Y_{t-1}) = \tilde{\epsilon}_t,$$

where $\tilde{\epsilon}_t = \begin{cases} \epsilon_t & \text{if } t \geq 0, \\ 0 & \text{otherwise.} \end{cases}$

This theorem provides a general representation valid for any VAR model and easily extendable to the case of a stationary process. We will now use it to further analyse the solutions of the multivariate rational expectations model and compare them to the solutions of the corresponding perfect foresight model.

4.2. Application to rational expectations models

(i) The model and its ARMA solutions Let us consider a general multivariate rational expectations model:

$$\sum_{h=0}^{H} \sum_{k=0}^{K} A_{kh} E[Y_{t+h-k} | I_{t-k}] = \epsilon_t.$$

In order to simplify the derivations, we choose a white noise as the right-hand side of the equation. Nevertheless, this assumption does not affect the generality of the results.

The corresponding perfect foresight model The perfect foresight model associated with the previous model is given by:

$$\sum_{h=0}^{H} \sum_{k=0}^{K} A_{kh} Y_{t+h-k} = \epsilon_t.$$

or equivalently by:

$$A(L)Y_t = \epsilon_t, \text{ with } A(L) = \sum_{h=0}^{H} \sum_{k=0}^{K} A_{kh} L^{k-h}.$$

It follows that the perfect foresight model is a VAR model (with a lagged noise).

From now on we assume that this model admits non-stationary solutions that are first-order integrated, written as:

$$(1-L)Y_t = H(L)\epsilon_{t-H}, \ t \geq 0.$$

In fact the perfect foresight model, as a VAR model, does not exhibit any particularity. The crucial point of our discussion concerns the comparison with the rational expectations model.

The linear solutions of the rational expectations model Let us now go back to the rational expectations model and consider its linear solutions, i.e. the solution having the following form:

$$Y_t = C(L)\epsilon_t, \ t \geq 0.$$

As we already know, the successive updating terms are given by $C_0 \epsilon_t$, $C_1 \epsilon_t, C_2 \epsilon_t, \ldots$, and the potential multiplicity comes from the arbitrariness of some of the components of the C_i's.

In any case, whatever the dimension of the solutions set, the general result of property (5.23) shows that the linear solutions of the rational expectations model are all solutions of the following equation:

$$\tilde{A}(L)Y_t = V_t, \ t \geq 0. \tag{5.30}$$

where the right-hand side V_t is a (finite) linear combination of the current and past values of the noise: $V_t = \Gamma(L)\epsilon_t$. The coefficients Γ_0,

$\Gamma_1, \ldots$ obviously depend on the choice of a particular solution that is made from the updating terms. But independently of that choice, Equation (5.30) may be rewritten in an equivalent way as:

$$(1 - L)Y_t = H(L)\Gamma(L)\epsilon_t, \quad t \geq 0. \tag{5.31}$$

Thus, as soon as the matrix $\Gamma(1)$ is regular, the kernel of $[H(1)\Gamma(1)]'$ coincides with the kernel of $[H(1)]'$. Since the cointegration concept is fundamentally based on this kernel, we may deduce the following result.

Property (5.32): The linear solutions of the rational expectations model for which $\Gamma(1)$ is regular[1] have the same properties with respect to cointegration as the solution of the corresponding perfect foresight model.

This result provides an interesting interpretation of the non-uniqueness phenomenon. Although there exist mostly multiple solutions, these have important common characteristics. More precisely all solutions satisfy the same long-term equilibrium relation. To some extent, the replacement of perfect foresight by rational expectations or the choice of a particular solution to the rational expectations model (instead of another one), only affects the part of the model which is concerned with describing the adjustments.

Nevertheless it remains that the solutions of the perfect foresight model are not always solutions to the rational expectations model. Thus different adjustments could arise under the perfect foresight assumption and the rationality assumption.

(ii) A representation theorem One may also easily obtain a representation theorem for rational expectations models. For this purpose, it suffices to rewrite the original model in the following form:

$$\tilde{A}(L)Y_t = \epsilon_{t-H} + \sum_{h=0}^{H} \sum_{k=0}^{K} A_{kh}(Y_{t+h-k+H} - E[Y_{t+h-k-H} | I_{t-k-H}]).$$

Then by using the extended version of the error correction representation given by Theorem (5.29), we have:

---

[1] The solutions corresponding to a singular $\Gamma(1)$ will admit more cointegration vectors than the other ones.

REDUCED FORMS OF RATIONAL EXPECTATIONS MODELS

$$\Delta\Omega'Y_t + \tilde{\Phi}(L)(Y_t - Y_{t-1}) - \sum_{h=0}^{H}\sum_{k=0}^{K} A_{kh}(Y_{t+h-k-H} - E[Y_{t+h-k-H}|I_{t-k-H}]) = \tilde{\epsilon}_{t-H}. \quad (5.33)$$

This expression clearly shows the diverse (stationary) elements that enter the adjustment relations:

— firstly the equilibrium error term: $\Omega'Y_t$;
— secondly the variable modifications: $Y_t - Y_{t-1}$;
— and lastly the rational prediction errors $Y_{t+h-k-H} - E[Y_{t+h-k-H}|I_{t-k-H}]$ that come from the specificity of the models we are concerned with.

(iii) An example In order to illustrate the previous results let us consider a two-dimensional model including rational expectations of future variables:

$$\Psi Y_t + E[Y_{t+1}|I_t] = \epsilon_t.$$

We take here, as autoregressive coefficient Ψ, a matrix having the following form:

$$\Psi = \begin{bmatrix} \Psi_{11} & \alpha(1 + \Psi_{11}) \\ \Psi_{21} & -1 + \alpha\Psi_{21} \end{bmatrix}, \quad \Psi_{11} \neq -1, \Psi_{21} \neq 0, \alpha \neq 0.$$

Non-stationarity In the general framework, we have defined $A(L)$ as the autoregressive matrix polynomial such that:

$$A(L) = \sum_{k=0}^{K}\sum_{h=0}^{H} A_{kh} L^{k-h},$$

In our particular case ($K = 0$, $H = 1$, $A_{00} = \Psi$, $A_{01} = 1$), we have:

$$A(L) = \Psi L + 1$$

$$= \begin{bmatrix} 1 + \psi_{11}L & \alpha(1 + \psi_{11})L \\ \psi_{21}L & 1 + (-1 + \alpha\psi_{21})L \end{bmatrix}.$$

The determinant of this matrix is given by:

$$\det A(L) = (1 + \psi_{11}L)(1 - L) + \alpha\psi_{21}L(1 + \psi_{11}L) - \alpha\psi_{21}L(1 + \psi_{11}L)$$
$$= (1 + \psi_{11}L)(1 - L).$$

It obviously has exactly one root equal to 1 since the elements of the adjoint matrix of A(L) are generally not divisible by $(1-L)$. Both series composing the endogenous vector-process are non-stationary and first-order integrated.

Cointegration We may now write the perfect foresight model associated with out model as follows:

$$(1+\psi_{11}L)(1-L)\begin{bmatrix}Y_{1t}\\Y_{2t}\end{bmatrix}=\begin{bmatrix}1+(-1+\alpha\psi_{21})L & -\alpha(1+\psi_{11})L\\-\psi_{21}L & 1+\psi_{11}L\end{bmatrix}L\,\epsilon_t,$$

or equivalently as:

$$(1-L)\begin{bmatrix}Y_{1t}\\Y_{2t}\end{bmatrix}=\frac{1}{1+\psi_{11}L}\begin{bmatrix}1+(-1+\alpha\psi_{21})L & -\alpha(1+\psi_{11})L\\-\psi_{21}L & 1+\psi_{11}L\end{bmatrix}L\,\epsilon_t$$
$$=H(L)\epsilon_t.$$

The moving-average matrix evaluated at 1 is given by:

$$H(1)=\frac{1}{1+\psi_{11}}\begin{bmatrix}\alpha\psi_{21} & -\alpha(1+\psi_{11})\\-\psi_{21} & 1+\psi_{11}\end{bmatrix}$$

The conditions $\psi_{11}\neq -1$ and $\psi_{21}\neq 0$ ensure that the rank of H(1) is equal to 1. Consequently the space of the cointegration vectors is generated by $\begin{bmatrix}1\\\alpha\end{bmatrix}$.

The error correction form In order to obtain the error correction form of the perfect foresight model, we rewrite the matrix A(L) in the following terms:

$$A(L)=\begin{bmatrix}1+\psi_{11}-\psi_{11}(1-L) & \alpha(1+\psi_{11})-\alpha(1+\psi_{11})(1-L)\\\psi_{21}-\psi_{21}(1-L) & \alpha\psi_{21}+(1-\alpha\psi_{21})(1-L)\end{bmatrix}.$$

From this expression, we immediately deduce the error correction form:

$$\begin{bmatrix}1+\psi_{11}\\\psi_{21}\end{bmatrix}(Y_{1t}+\alpha Y_{2t})-\begin{bmatrix}\psi_{11} & \alpha(1+\psi_{11})\\-\psi_{21} & \alpha\psi_{21}-1\end{bmatrix}(Y_t-Y_{t-1})=\tilde{\epsilon}_{t-1}. \quad (5.34)$$

The rational expectations model The rational expectations model is given by:

$$\Psi Y_t+E[Y_{t+1}|I_t]=\epsilon_t.$$

Along the lines of the reduction method, it may be shown that the general solution of this model is provided by:

$$A(L)Y_t = \epsilon_t^0 + \epsilon_{t-1}, \tag{5.35}$$

where ϵ^0 denotes an arbitrary two-dimensional martingale difference.

If we restrict ourselves to the linear solutions, we have:

$$A(L)Y_t = C\epsilon_t + \epsilon_{t-1},$$

where $C = \begin{bmatrix} C_{11} & C_{12} \\ C_{21} & C_{22} \end{bmatrix}$ is a matrix from which elements may be chosen arbitrarily. The latter system is equivalent to:

$$(1-L)Y_t = H(L)(C + \text{Id } L)\epsilon_t.$$

In order to analyse the cointegration problem for this case, we must consider the rank of the matrix $H(1)(C + \text{Id})$. As we know that the rank of $H(1)$ is equal to 1, the previous matrix may have either a rank equal to 1, or a rank equal to 0. Mostly the rank of $H(1)(C + \text{Id})$ is equal to 1. Consequently the space of the cointegration vectors is of dimension 1 and is generated by the vector $\begin{bmatrix} 1 \\ \alpha \end{bmatrix}$.

However it could happen that the rank is equal to zero. This corresponds to the case where: $H(1)(C + \text{Id}) = 0$. By expanding the preceding equation, we obtain:

$$\frac{1}{1+\psi_{11}} \begin{bmatrix} -\alpha \\ 1 \end{bmatrix} (-\psi_{21}, 1+\psi_{11}) \begin{bmatrix} C_{11}+1 & C_{12} \\ C_{21} & C_{22}+1 \end{bmatrix} = 0,$$

or equivalently:

$$\begin{cases} -\psi_{21}(C_{11}+1) + (1+\psi_{11})C_{21} = 0 \\ -\psi_{21}C_{12} + (1+\psi_{11})(C_{21}+1) = 0. \end{cases}$$

Thus among the infinity of linear solution of rational expectations models, some may reveal stationary and lead to a cointegration space of dimension 2. Nevertheless, this case only occurs in a subset of solutions that has a zero-measure in the set of the linear solutions.

On the other hand, an error correction representation may be obtained for the general solution of the model. It is deduced from System (5.35):

$$\begin{bmatrix} 1+\psi_{11} \\ \psi_{21} \end{bmatrix} (Y_{1t} + \alpha Y_{2t}) - \begin{bmatrix} \psi_{11} & \alpha(1+\psi_{11}) \\ \psi_{21} & \alpha\psi_{21} - 1 \end{bmatrix} (Y_t - Y_{t-1}) - \epsilon_t^0 = \epsilon_{t-1}.$$

Furthermore, since ϵ_t^0 is interpreted as the rational prediction error made in forecasting Y_t at time $t-1$, we may rewrite the previous system as:

$$\begin{bmatrix} 1+\psi_{11} \\ \psi_{21} \end{bmatrix}(Y_{1t}+\alpha Y_{2t}) - \begin{bmatrix} \psi_{11} & \alpha(1+\psi_{11}) \\ \psi_{21} & \alpha\psi_{21}-1 \end{bmatrix}(Y_t - Y_{t-1})$$
$$- (Y_t - E[Y_t | I_{t-1}]) = \epsilon_{t-1}.$$

Finally, for the linear solution corresponding to the choice of a prediction error in one relation with ϵ (C is invertible), it is even possible to derive a representation which no longer includes an error term:

$$\begin{bmatrix} 1+\psi_{11} \\ \psi_{21} \end{bmatrix}(Y_{1t}+\alpha Y_{2t}) - \begin{bmatrix} \psi_{11} & \alpha(1+\psi_{11}) \\ \psi_{21} & \alpha\psi_{21}-1 \end{bmatrix}(Y_t - Y_{t-1})$$
$$- (Y_t - E[Y_t | I_{t-1}]) - C^{-1}(Y_{t-1} - E[Y_{t-1} | I_{t-2}]) = 0.$$

5. Concluding remarks

In the preceding sections, solutions of rational expectations models were derived. We started with the case of univariate models with current or future expectations. We then generalized the results to the case of multivariate models. This led us to describe the problem of multiple solutions and to characterize the dimension of the set of solutions in terms of the structural parameters of the model.

Models involving a continuum of equilibria lead to several difficulties: Which is the solution consistent with facts? How does one deal with simulating, estimating and testing such models? Etc. Two avenues, at least, can be followed to tackle these questions.

First, one can look for properties and procedures which do not depend on the solution(s) that hold at least for a wide range of them. Robust properties are discussed in the literature, e.g. the possibility to provide consistent estimators of structural parameters, without explicitly giving the solution. The number of cases in which such properties do exist is however limited.

A second approach would be to make better use of economic theory and of the restrictions it imposes on the resulting (supply and demand) equations; such restrictions may sometimes turn out to be sufficient to ensure uniqueness. Such an approach has not yet been systematically explored.

Finally, inference problems, which are completely ignored in this monograph, lead to very interesting issues among others, the study of relations between the existence of consistent estimators and the dimension of the solution set; the identification of parameters; the possibility to provide consistent estimators of structural parameters, without explicit solution; direct (without structural model) or indirect (model based) tests of the rational expectations hypothesis.

References

Aoki, M. and M. Canzoneri (1979): "Reduced forms of rational expectations models", *Quarterly Journal of Economics*, **93**, 59-71.
Broze, L., C. Gouriéroux and A. Szafarz (1989): "Computation of multipliers in multivariate rational expectations models", Discussion Paper, ULB.
Davidson, R. (1986): "Cointegration in linear dynamic systems", Discussion Paper, London School of Economics.
Davidson, J., D. Hendry, F. Srba and S. Yeo (1978): "Econometric modelling of the aggregate time series relationship between consumer's expenditure and income in the United Kingdom", *Economic Journal*, **88**, 661-692.
Engle, R. and C. Granger (1987): "Cointegration and error correction: representation, estimation and testing", *Econometrica*, **55**, 251-276.
Engle, R. and M. Watson (1985): "The Kalman filter: Applications to forecasting and rational expectations model", in *Advances in Econometrics, Fifth World Congress*, T. Bewley (ed.), Cambridge University Press.
Granger, C. (1981): "Some properties of time series data and their use in econometric model specification", *Journal of Econometrics*, **16**, 251-276.
Granger, C. (1986): "Development in the study of cointegrated economic variables", *Oxford Bulletin of Economics and Statistics*, **48**, 213-228.
Hunter, J. (1988): "Cointegration, rational expectations and error correction", Discussion Paper, University of Surrey.
Kollintzas, T. (1985): "The symmetric linear rational expectations model", *Econometrica*, **53**, 963-976.
METRIC (1977): "METRIC, modèle économétriel trimestriel de la conjoncture", *Annales de l'INSEE*, 26-27.
Palm, F. and G. Pfann (1988): "Interrelation, exogenous shocks and cointegration in a multivariate adjustment rational expectations model", Discussion Paper, University of Limburg, Maastricht.
Pesaran, M. (1981): "Solution of linear rational expectations models", *Journal of Econometrics*, **16**, 375-398.
Pesaran, M. H. (1987): *The Limits to Rational Expectations*, Basil Blackwell, Oxford.
Wallis, K. (1980): "Econometric implications of the rational expectations hypothesis", *Econometrica*, **48**, 49-73.
Watson, M. (1986): "Recursive solution methods for dynamic linear rational expectations models", Discussion Paper, Northwestern University.
Wegge, L. (1984): "Identifiability of structural models containing Muth-rational current and future expectations", Discussion Paper 233, University of California, Davis.
Wegge, L. (1984): "The canonical form of the dynamic Muth-rational future expectations model", Discussion Paper, University of California, Davis.
Whiteman, C. (1983): *Linear Rational Expectations Models: A User's Guide*, Minneapolis, University of Minnesota Press.

6. A MEAN-VARIANCE MODEL

In this section, we study the evolution of the equilibrium price of a good (coffee, for instance) that can be traded for speculative purposes and used for consumption. However, the focus is on the effects of speculative trading, hence we specify a very simple excess supply function for the good. The speculative demands are derived from the portofolio choice problem of risk averse traders who can invest in a risky and a riskless asset. We then derive explicit forms of equilibrium paths and dicuss the effects of various factors on the amplitude of the risk premium.

The model we consider is related to previous works by Grossman (1976), Danthine (1978), Kawai (1983). The speculators' maximization of constant absolute risk aversion utility function leads to a dynamic stochastic mean-variance model that includes rational expectations.

The introduction of nonlinearities makes the resolution of the model much harder. Therefore, as a first step in our analysis, we extend to mean-variance rational expectations models the solution method developed in the previous sections for the linear case. From the expressions of equilibrium paths that we obtain, it is possible to derive some interesting properties concerning the importance of the risk premium.

1. The model

The basic model includes two assets that can be traded at each point of time. The first asset is riskless. It has a price fixed to unity and pays r "dollars" at the end of each period. This constant return r ($r > 0$) is assumed to be known by everyone. The second asset, considered as risky, takes the form of a material good storable for speculative purposes, that may be bought at the beginning of period t at unit price p_t and sold at the end of the period at a new price p_{t+1} (unknown at time t).

The complete specification of the model will be given by setting the demand function of the speculators and the excess supply function for the storable good.

1.1. Demand function of the speculators

To describe the evolution of the traders' portofolios, we follow the usual approach based on the optimization of an expected utility function conditional on the currently available information. We assume that all the traders have the same endowments, preferences and beliefs. We consider thus the case of a single agent.

At the end of period $t-1$, the agent is endowed with stocks of the two types of assets: M_{t-1} for the riskless asset and X_{t-1} for the risky one. At the beginning of period t, these assets may be sold and a new portofolio is composed. The wealth is given by:

$$W_t = p_t X_{t-1} + R M_{t-1},$$

where $R = 1 + r$.

Let (M_t, X_t) denote the new portofolio. The budget constraint is then:

$$W_t = p_t X_{t-1} + R M_{t-1} = p_t X_t + M_t. \tag{6.1}$$

To determine the allocation (M_t, X_t) the agent has a myopic optimization behavior: the expected utility is maximized one period ahead with reference to a non-decreasing concave utility function $U(W_t)$ depending only on wealth.

Let I_t denote the available information. The agent's behavior is summarized by the following program:

$$\left.\begin{array}{l} \underset{X_t, M_t}{\text{Max}} \ E[U(W_{t+1})|I_t] = E[U(p_{t+1}X_t + RM_t)|I_t] \\ \text{s.t.:} \ p_t X_t + M_t = W_t \end{array}\right\} \tag{6.2}$$

Generally such a program has no explicit solution. Therefore we specify an exponential form for the utility function:

$$U(W_t) = -\exp(-\eta W_t), \tag{6.3}$$

where η ($\eta > 0$), the coefficient of absolute risk aversion, is assumed constant. The expected utility only depends on the conditional distribution of the future price p_{t+1} given the information set I_t. With a normal conditional distribution, the expected utility only depends on the conditional mean $E[p_{t+1}|I_t]$ and the conditional variance $V[p_{t+1}|I_t]$ (equal to the residual variance). More precisely, normality implies:

$$E[U(W_{t+1})|I_t] = -\exp\left(-\eta E[W_{t+1}|I_t] + \frac{\eta^2}{2} V[W_{t+1}|I_t]\right)$$
$$= -\exp\left(-\eta(E[p_{t+1}|I_t]X_t + RM_t) + \frac{\eta^2}{2} X_t^2 V[p_{t+1}|I_t]\right).$$

Taking into account the budget constraint (6.1), we can substitute for one of the quantities, say $M_t = W_t - p_t X_t$, and obtain from (6.4):

$$E[U(W_{t+1})|I_t]$$
$$= -\exp\left(-\eta(X_t(E[p_{t+1}|I_t] - Rp_t) + RW_t) + \frac{\eta^2}{2} X_t^2 V[p_{t+1}|I_t]\right).$$

Writing the first-order condition yields a demand function for the risky asset:

$$X_t = \frac{E[p_{t+1}|I_t] - Rp_t}{\eta V[p_{t+1}|I_t]}. \tag{6.5}$$

From now on this particular form of the demand function will be used. It is restrictive for two obvious reasons. Firstly, it only depends on the transition between the past and the future by means of the conditional mean and variance. Secondly, the traders' demand does not depend on the wealth W_t. These restrictions afford decisive advantages in terms of the tractability of the model. Indeed the demand only depends on current expectations $E[p_{t+1}|I_t]$, $V[p_{t+1}|I_t]$ instead of both current and lagged expectations $E[p_{t+1}|I_{t-j}]$, $V[p_{t+1}|I_{t-j}]$, $j = 0, 1, 2, \ldots$

However, specification (6.5) of the demand is sufficiently flexible to take into account risk aversion and leads to a model in which the *certainty equivalent principle* does not apply.

1.2. Excess supply function of storable good

The net supply of the storable good is the sum of the previous stock X_{t-1} and the excess of current production Q_t over domestic demand C_t. This excess supply can be deduced from producers' and consumers' behaviors. We take here a simple description of this excess supply function assuming linearity, with respect to the current price:

$$Q_t - C_t = \alpha p_t + u_t, \quad \alpha > 0, \tag{6.6}$$

where u denotes an exogenous stochastic process summarizing all the stochastic factors that affect production and domestic demand at time t.

1.3. Equilibrium condition

For the risky asset, the equilibrium condition at time t is:

$$X_t = X_{t-1} + Q_t - C_t.$$

Since the demand function X_t and the excess supply $Q_t - C_t$ are specified respectively by Equations (6.5) and (6.6), this condition becomes:

$$\frac{E[p_{t+1}|I_t] - R p_t}{\eta V[p_{t+1}|I_t]} = \frac{E[p_{t+1}|I_{t-1}] - R p_{t-1}}{\eta V[p_t|I_{t-1}]} + \alpha p_t + u_t. \quad (6.7)$$

An equilibrium price path is thus defined as a stochastic process $(p_t)_{t>0}$ satisfying Equation (6.7) for any non-negative value of t.

2. Evolution of the equilibrium price

Equation (6.7) is the starting point of the description of the equilibrium price paths. It is a dynamic rational expectation model including *non-linearities* due to the presence of conditional variances.

The following result gives the set of all equilibrium price paths satisfying Equation (6.7).

Property (6.8): Any solution of the system of equilibrium conditions (6.7) satisfies the difference equation:

$$\frac{p_{t+1} - \epsilon_{t+1}^0 + R p_t}{\eta E[(\epsilon_{t+1}^0)^2|I_t]} = \frac{p_t - \epsilon_t^0 - R p_{t-1}}{\eta E[(\epsilon_t^0)^2|I_{t-1}]} + \alpha p_t + u_t, \quad (6.9)$$

where ϵ^0 is an arbitrary martingale difference.

The proof of this property is similar to the one developed in the linear case (see Broze, Gouriéroux and Szafarz (1988)). In particular, ϵ_t^0 can be interpreted as the error made in forecasting the equilibrium price:

$$\epsilon_t^0 = p_t - E[p_t|I_{t-1}].$$

It is interesting to note that property (6.8) is valid without any assumption on the stochastic structure of the exogenous process u and without any restriction concerning the solutions. Mean-variance rational expectations models are often solved under the assumption that the conditional variance of the price $V[p_{t+1}|I_t]$ is time-independent (see for instance Kawai (1983)). Under this additional condition the study of a mean-variance model is similar to the analysis of a linear rational expectations model and the risk aversion feature disappears. To illustrate the consequences of this stationarity restriction on the second order moment, consider the simple case where the exogenous process u is a sequence of independent and identically distributed variables, with mean m and variance σ^2.

A subset of all possible prediction errors is given by:

$$\epsilon_t^0 = f(t)(u_t - m),$$

where f is any deterministic function. The process ϵ^0 is a martingale difference since:

$$\begin{aligned}E[\epsilon_{t+1}^0 | I_t] &= E[f(t+1)(u_{t+1} - m) | I_t] \\ &= f(t+1)E[(u_{t+1} - m) | I_t] \\ &= 0.\end{aligned}$$

Since f is an arbitrary function, the mean-variance model is compatible with any kind of time heteroscedasticity of the price. Furthermore, even if the solutions considered are restricted to those having a constant conditional variance, the value of this constant $V[p_{t+1} | I_t]$ is fixed by the model (since p_t is endogenous) and therefore it cannot be taken as an additional structural parameter.

3. Risk premia

3.1. *Asymptotic behavior of the solutions*

Consider a totally risk averse agent in the sense that the parameter $\eta = \infty$. Consequently, the portofolio only contains the safe asset. One unit of this asset hold at time 0 gives a return R^t at time t.

Symmetrically a (money) unit of the risky asset hold at time 0 gives a stochastic return of p_t/p_0. Since it is natural for agents holding the risky asset to benefit from a *risk premium*, one may intuitively expect that the ratio p_t/p_0 will (on average) be larger than R^t. Moreover, since agents' expectations have a direct effect on the price level, one may also hypothesize that the more risk averse is the trader, the higher is the discrepancy between the ratio p_t/p_0 and the certain return R^t.

We now proceed to a formal analysis of these ideas. To simplify the presentation, we assume that the exogenous process u has an asymptotically stationary moving average representation:

$$u_t = m + h(L)\tilde{\epsilon}_t, \tag{6.11}$$

where m is the mean of u_t ($\forall t \geq 0$) and $\tilde{\epsilon}$ is an independent white noise with variance σ^2. The values of $\tilde{\epsilon}_t$ associated with negative indices are fixed to zero.

We also restrict the analysis to solutions having the following form:

$$p_t = \mu_t + C(L)\tilde{\epsilon}_t = \mu_t + \sum_{j=0}^{t} C_j \tilde{\epsilon}_{t-j}, \quad (6.12)$$

where μ_t is the time-dependent mean of the price.

This class of processes is rather large. It may contain stationary as well as non-stationary solutions. Non-stationarity may appear not only through the mean, but also through the moving average coefficients since the sequence (C_j) is not necessarily summable. The previous restrictions have the advantage of providing a large parametric class of solutions, which is described in Broze, Gouriéroux and Szafarz (1988).

Property (6.13): The equilibrium price paths having the following representation:

$$p_t = \mu_t + C(L)\tilde{\epsilon}_t,$$

are such that $C(L)$ verifies:

$$C(L) = \frac{C_0 - C_0 L + L h(L)\eta C_0^2 \sigma^2}{1 - [1 + R + \alpha\eta C_0^2 \sigma^2]L + RL^2}$$

and the sequence (μ_t) verifies:

$$\mu_{t+1} - (R + 1 + \alpha\eta C_0^2 \sigma^2)\mu_t + R\mu_{t-1} = \eta C_0^2 \sigma^2 m, \quad t \geq 0,$$

where the value of C_0 may be chosen arbitrarily.

A price increase greater than R^t may be described in two different ways, through the mean and/or through the stochastic part $C(L)\tilde{\epsilon}_t$. In fact, if $h(L)$ has the form of a rational operator, the same is true for $C(L)$:

$$C(L) = \frac{\Theta(L)}{\Phi(L)}.$$

Although the mean of the stochastic part is always zero, unstable roots of $\Phi(L)$ might have great effects on the variability of prices. More precisely, to study the price increase through the stochastic part, one has to check whether $\Phi(L)$ has roots lying in the unit circle that are smaller than $1/R$.

We have to study the behavior of the trend μ_t and of the stochastic part $C(L)\tilde{\epsilon}_t$. However, both may be analyzed together because the difference equation satisfied by the mean price is:

$$\Phi^*(L)\mu_{t+1} = (1 - (R + 1 + \alpha\eta C_0^2 \sigma^2)L + RL^2)\mu_{t+1} = \eta C_0^2 \sigma^2 m,$$

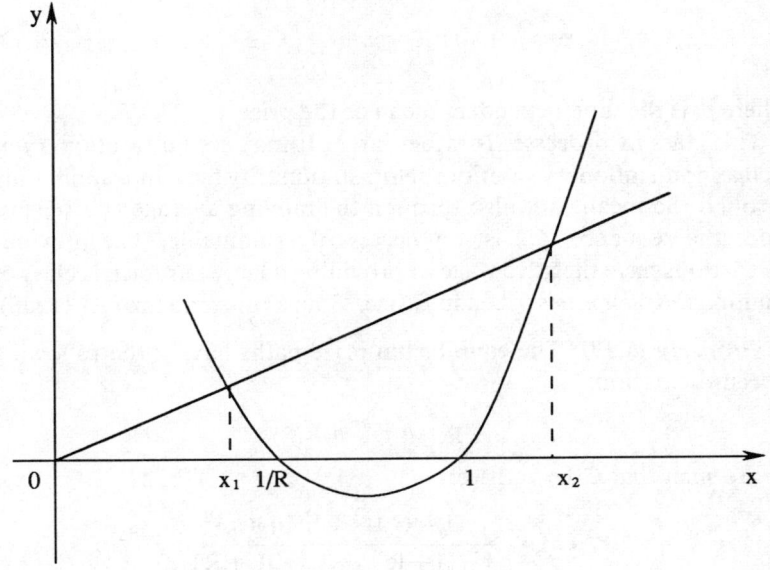

FIGURE 9

and $\Phi^*(L)$ and $\Phi(L)$ have the same roots outside the unit circle. Thus divergent trend and variance occur simultaneously according to the values taken by the roots of the following equation:

$$\Phi^*(x) = R x^2 - (R + 1 + \alpha\eta C_0^2\sigma^2)x + 1 = 0.$$

This equation is equivalent to:

$$\alpha\eta C_0^2\sigma^2 x = (1-x)(1-Rx).$$

Since $\eta > 0$, $R \geq 1$ and $\alpha > 0$, the curves given by $y = \alpha\eta C_0^2\sigma^2 x$ and $y = (1-x)(1-Rx)$ are given by Figure 9. Consequently, the roots x_1 and x_2 of the equation are real and such that:

$$0 \leq x_1 \leq \frac{1}{R} \leq 1 \leq x_2.$$

Thus, except in the case where suitable initial conditions give a constant sequence $\mu = \mu_t$ $\forall t$, *and* where C_0 is chosen so that the explosive root of

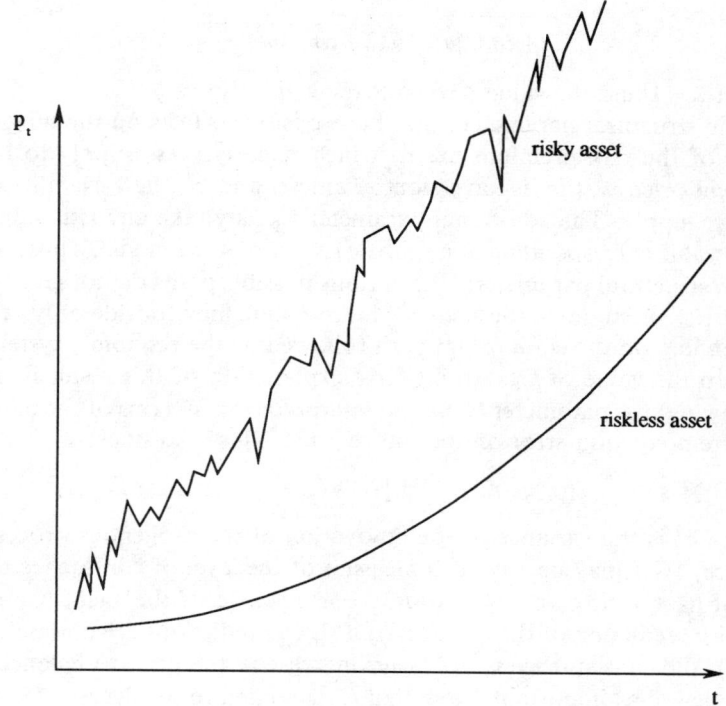

FIGURE 10

$\phi^*(L)$ cancels with a corresponding root of $\Theta(L)$, any solution: $p_t = \mu_t + C(L)\tilde{\epsilon}_t$, asymptotically increases with rate $(1/x_1)^t$, i.e. faster than the return on the riskless asset (see Figure 10).

3.2. Comparative statics

The ratio R^{-1}/x_1 may be viewed as a natural index of the asymptotic importance of the risk premium. This ratio is:

$$C(\alpha, \eta, C_0^2, \sigma^2, R) = \frac{2}{1 + R + \alpha\eta C_0^2 \sigma^2 - \sqrt{(1 + R + \alpha\eta C_0^2 \sigma^2)^2 - 4R}}$$

This index takes value from 1 to $+\infty$. It increases with α, η, C_0^2 and σ^2, and depends negatively on R. It takes the value:

$$\frac{2}{2 + \alpha\eta C_0^2 \sigma^2 - \sqrt{(2 + \alpha\eta C_0^2 \sigma^2)^2 - 4}}$$

when R = 1 and the value 1 when R tends to infinity.

The structural parameters that have positive effects on the magnitude of the risk premium are α, which relates excess supply to the current price, η, the risk aversion parameter and σ^2, the variability of excess supply. The additional parameter C_0 may take any real value, each value corresponding to a specific solution of the model. Thus, for given structural parameters, the various possible paths do not give the same risk premium to the agents. This premium may considerably vary depending on the equilibrium path followed by the economic system, i.e. on the value of C_0. An intuitive explanation of this result is the following: the parameter C_0 has an interpretation in terms of the mean square prediction error on the future price. This is so since:

$$V(p_{t+1} - E[p_{t+1}|I_t]) = V(C_0\tilde{\epsilon}_{t+1}) = C_0^2\sigma^2,$$

where σ^2 is the variance of the innovation of the exogenous process. Hence, $|C_0|$ may be seen as a measure of the level of confidence the agent has in his own expectations. For instance, if the agent has no precise prediction of the price (even if these predictions are optimal *ex post*), the consequence is the faster increase in the price to balance a risk viewed as important. Note that C_0 is related to the degree of confidence in his prediction and not to the structural variability of the exogenous environment. The latter is captured by the value of σ^2.

This section was exclusively devoted to a mean-variance model. It is obvious that one should consider analyzing nonlinear models which are more general than the latter; in doing so, one has however to bear in mind that, even without introducing expectations, the behavior of such models is complex and their solution(s) may exhibit chaos and bifurcations.

Nevertheless, a full analysis of some specific models could prove useful: indeed, in some cases, nonlinearities may lead to a finite number of (isolated) equilibria, even with future expectations. Also, there could be cases in which, even in the presence of chaos, solutions are endowed with the same type of ergodic properties; for instance, one could make use of observed distributions of successive observations corresponding to a solution, converging to a value independent of this solution.

References

Blanchard, O. and M. Watson (1982): "Bubbles, rational expectations and financial markets", in *Crises in the Economic and Financial Structure*, P. Wachtel (ed.), Lexington Books.
Broze, L., C. Gouriéroux and A. Szafarz (1988): "Speculative bubbles and exchange of information on the market of a storable good", in *Economic Complexity: Chaos, Sunspots, Bubbles and Nonlinearity*, W. Barnett, J. Geweke and K. Shell (eds), Cambridge University Press.
Danthine, J. P. (1978): "Information, future prices and stabilizing speculation", *Journal of Economic Theory*, **17**, 79-98.
Fair, R. and J. Taylor (1983): "Solution and maximum likelihood estimation of dynamic non-linear rational expectations models", *Econometrica*, **51**, 1169-1184.
Grossman, S. J. (1976): "On the efficiency of comparative stock markets where traders have diverse information", *Journal of Finance*, **31**, 573-585.
Grossman, S. J. (1981): "An introduction to the theory of rational expectations under asymmetric information", *Review of Economic Studies*, **48**, 541-559.
Grossman, S. J. and J. E. Stiglitz (1980): "On the impossibility of informationally efficient markets", *American Economic Review*, **70**, 393-408.
Hansen, L. P. and K. J. Singleton (1982): "Generalized instrumental variables estimation of non-linear rational expectations models", *Econometrica*, **50**, 1269-1286.
Hellwig, M. F. (1982): "Rational expectations equilibrium with conditioning on past prices: A mean-variance example", *Journal of Economic Theory*, **26**, 435-459.
Kawai, M. (1983): "Price volatility of storable commodities under rational expectations in spot and future markets", *International Economic Review*, **24**, 435-459.

INDEX

Adaptive expectation 8
Adjoint operator method 92, 96
ARIMA solutions 103

Backward solution 47

Cagan model 38, 76, 78, 85
Canonical forms 89
Cointegrated 101
Cointegration 99, 100
Cointegration vector 101
Conditional expectation 12
Conditional variance 111
Constraints on updating terms 75
Current expectations model 68, 71

Degree of multiplicity 97
Direct effect 30, 70

Equilibrium error term 102
Error correction 9
Error correction form 101
Error correction representation 102
Expectation scheme 6, 28
Explosive part 100
Exponential smoothing 11
Extrapolative form 11

Forward solution 45
Future expectations model 70, 71

General model 89
General solution 44, 54, 81, 85, 88, 96, 107, 108
General univariate model 73

Homogeneous equation 54
Horizon 7
Hyperinflation models 37

Indirect effect 30, 70
Information set 6
Initial condition 57

Law of iterated predictions 15
Learning processes 34, 63
Linear solutions 48, 79, 103
Linear stationary solutions 52, 98
Long-term equilibrium relation 102

Martingale 16
Martingale difference 16
Mean-variance model 110
Multivariate models 82
Muth model 24, 78

Naive expectation 9
Non-stationary solutions 98
Nonlinearities 113

Optimal prediction 12

Perfect foresight 9
Prediction error 6, 16
Predictions 6
Processes 7

Rational expectation 12
Reduced form 25, 27, 40, 78, 86
Recursive case 86
Risk premium 110, 114

Smoothing 8
Stationary part 100
Stationary solutions 60
Structural matrix 85, 86, 94
Successive predictions 7
Sunspots 59

Taylor model 39, 78
Terminal condition 57

Undetermined coefficients procedure 50
Updating 8, 16

Variance analysis equation 14
VAR 99

FUNDAMENTALS OF PURE AND APPLIED ECONOMICS

SECTIONS AND EDITORS

BALANCE OF PAYMENTS AND INTERNATIONAL FINANCE
W. Branson, Princeton University

DISTRIBUTION
A. Atkinson, London School of Economics

ECONOMIC DEVELOPMENT STUDIES
S. Chakravarty, Delhi School of Economics

ECONOMIC HISTORY
P. David, Stanford University, and M. Lévy-Leboyer, Université Paris X

ECONOMIC SYSTEMS
J.M. Montias, Yale University

ECONOMICS OF HEALTH, EDUCATION, POVERTY AND CRIME
V. Fuchs, Stanford University

ECONOMICS OF THE HOUSEHOLD AND INDIVIDUAL BEHAVIOR
J. Muellbauer, University of Oxford

ECONOMICS OF TECHNOLOGICAL CHANGE
F. M. Scherer, Harvard University

EVOLUTION OF ECONOMIC STRUCTURES, LONG-TERM MODELS, PLANNING POLICY, INTERNATIONAL ECONOMIC STRUCTURES
W. Michalski, O.E.C.D., Paris

EXPERIMENTAL ECONOMICS
C. Plott, California Institute of Technology

GOVERNMENT OWNERSHIP AND REGULATION OF ECONOMIC ACTIVITY
E. Bailey, Carnegie-Mellon University, USA

INTERNATIONAL ECONOMIC ISSUES
B. Balassa, The World Bank

INTERNATIONAL TRADE
M. Kemp, University of New South Wales

LABOR AND ECONOMICS
F. Welch, University of California, Los Angeles, and J. Smith, The Rand Corporation

MACROECONOMIC THEORY
J. Grandmont, CEPREMAP, Paris

MARXIAN ECONOMICS
J. Roemer, University of California, Davis
NATURAL RESOURCES AND ENVIRONMENTAL ECONOMICS
C. Henry, Ecole Polytechnique, Paris
ORGANIZATION THEORY AND ALLOCATION PROCESSES
A. Postlewaite, University of Pennsylvania
POLITICAL SCIENCE AND ECONOMICS
J. Ferejohn, Stanford University
PROGRAMMING METHODS IN ECONOMICS
M. Balinski, Ecole Polytechnique, Paris
PUBLIC EXPENDITURES
P. Dasgupta, University of Cambridge
REGIONAL AND URBAN ECONOMICS
R. Arnott, Queen's University, Canada
SOCIAL CHOICE THEORY
A. Sen, Harvard University
TAXES
R. Guesnerie, Ecole des Hautes Etudes en Sciences Sociales, Paris
THEORY OF THE FIRM AND INDUSTRIAL ORGANIZATION
A. Jacquemin, Université Catholique de Louvain

FUNDAMENTALS OF PURE AND APPLIED ECONOMICS

PUBLISHED TITLES

Volume 1 (International Trade Section)
GAME THEORY IN INTERNATIONAL ECONOMICS
by John McMillan

Volume 2 (Marxian Economics Section)
MONEY, ACCUMULATION AND CRISIS
BY Duncan K. Foley

Volume 3 (Theory of the Firm and Industrial Organization Section)
DYNAMIC MODELS OF OLIGOPOLY
by Drew Fudenberg and Jean Tirole

Volume 4 (Marxian Economics Section)
VALUE, EXPLOITATION AND CLASS
by John E. Roemer

Volume 5 (Regional and Urban Economics Section)
LOCATION THEORY
by Jean Jaskold Gabszewicz and Jacques-François Thisse, Masahisa Fujita, and Urs Schweizer

Volume 6 (Political Science and Economics Section)
MODELS OF IMPERFECT INFORMATION IN POLITICS
by Randall L. Calvert

Volume 7 (Marxian Economics Section)
CAPITALIST IMPERIALISM, CRISIS AND THE STATE
by John Willoughby

Volume 8 (Marxian Economics Section)
MARXISM AND "REALLY EXISTING SOCIALISM"
by Alec Nove

Volume 9 (Economic Systems Section)
THE NONPROFIT ENTERPRISE IN MARKET ECONOMIES
by Estelle James and Susan Rose-Ackerman

Volume 10 (Regional and Urban Economics Section)
URBAN PUBLIC FINANCE
by David E. Wildasin

Volume 11 (Regional and Urban Economics Section)
URBAN DYNAMICS AND URBAN EXTERNALITIES
by Takahiro Miyao and Yoshitsugu Kanemoto

Volume 12 (Marxian Economics Section)
DEVELOPMENT AND MODES OF PRODUCTION IN MARXIAN ECONOMICS: A CRITICAL EVALUATION
by Alan Richards

Volume 13 (Economics of Technological Change Section)
TECHNOLOGICAL CHANGE AND PRODUCTIVITY GROWTH
by Albert N. Link

Volume 14 (Economic Systems Section)
ECONOMICS OF COOPERATION AND THE LABOR-MANAGED ECONOMY
by John P. Bonin and Louis Putterman

Volume 15 (International Trade Section)
UNCERTAINTY AND THE THEORY OF INTERNATIONAL TRADE
by Earl L. Grinols

Volume 16 (Theory of the Firm and Industrial Organization Section)
THE CORPORATION: GROWTH, DIVERSIFICATION AND MERGERS
by Dennis C. Mueller

Volume 17 (Economics of Technological Change Section)
MARKET STRUCTURE AND TECHNOLOGICAL CHANGE
by William L. Baldwin and John T. Scott

Volume 18 (Social Choice Theory Section)
INTERPROFILE CONDITIONS AND IMPOSSIBILITY
by Peter C. Fishburn

Volume 19 (Macroeconomic Theory Section)
WAGE AND EMPLOYMENT PATTERNS IN LABOR CONTRACTS: MICROFOUNDATIONS AND MACROECONOMIC IMPLICATIONS
by Russell W. Cooper

Volume 20 (Government Ownership and Regulation of Economic Activity Section)
DESIGNING REGULATORY POLICY WITH LIMITED INFORMATION
by David Besanko and David E. M. Sappington

Volume 21 (Economics of Technological Change Section)
THE ROLE OF DEMAND AND SUPPLY IN THE GENERATION AND DIFFUSION OF TECHNICAL CHANGE
by Colin G. Thirtle and Vernon W. Ruttan

Volume 22 (Regional and Urban Economics Section)
SYSTEMS OF CITIES AND FACILITY LOCATION
by Pierre Hansen, Martine Labbé, Dominique Peeters and Jacques-François Thisse, and J. Vernon Henderson

Volume 23 (International Trade Section)
DISEQUILIBRIUM TRADE THEORIES
by Motoshige Itoh and Takashi Negishi

Volume 24 (Balance of Payments and International Finance Section)
THE EMPIRICAL EVIDENCE ON THE EFFICIENCY OF FORWARD AND FUTURES FOREIGN EXCHANGE MARKETS
by Robert J. Hodrick

Volume 25 (Economic Systems Section)
THE COMPARATIVE ECONOMICS OF RESEARCH DEVELOPMENT AND INNOVATION IN EAST AND WEST: A SURVEY
by Philip Hanson and Keith Pavitt

Volume 26 (Regional and Urban Economics Section)
MODELING IN URBAN AND REGIONAL ECONOMICS
By Alex Anas

Volume 27 (Economic Systems Section)
FOREIGN TRADE IN THE CENTRALLY PLANNED ECONOMY
by Thomas A. Wolf

Volume 28 (Theory of the Firm and Industrial Organization Section)
MARKET STRUCTURE AND PERFORMANCE – THE EMPIRICAL RESEARCH
by John S. Cubbin

Volume 29 (Economic Development Studies Section)
STABILIZATION AND GROWTH IN DEVELOPING COUNTRIES: A STRUCTURALIST APPROACH
by Lance Taylor

Volume 30 (Economics of Technological Change Section)
THE ECONOMICS OF THE PATENT SYSTEM
by Erich Kaufer

Volume 31 (Regional and Urban Economics Section)
THE ECONOMICS OF HOUSING MARKETS
by Richard F. Muth and Allen C. Goodman

Volume 32 (International Trade Section)
THE POLITICAL ECONOMY OF PROTECTION
by Arye L. Hillman

Volume 33 (Natural Resources and Environmental Economics Section)
NON-RENEWABLE RESOURCES EXTRACTION PROGRAMS AND MARKETS
by John M. Hartwick

Volume 34 (Government Ownership and Regulation of Economic Activity Section)
A PRIMER ON ENVIRONMENTAL POLICY DESIGN
by Robert W. Hahn

Volume 35 (Economics of Technological Change Section)
TWENTY-FIVE CENTURIES OF TECHNOLOGICAL CHANGE
by Joel Mokyr

Volume 36 (Government Ownership and Regulation of Economic Activity Section)
PUBLIC ENTERPRISE IN MONOPOLISTIC AND OLIGOPOLISTIC INDUSTRIES
by Ingo Vogelsang

Volume 37 (Economic Development Studies Section)
AGRARIAN STRUCTURE AND ECONOMIC UNDERDEVELOPMENT
by Kaushik Basu

Volume 38 (Macroeconomic Theory Section)
MACROECONOMIC POLICY, CREDIBILITY AND POLITICS
by Torsten Persson and Guido Tabellini

Volume 39 (Economic History Section)
TOPOLOGY OF INDUSTRIALIZATION PROCESSES IN THE NINETEENTH CENTURY
by Sidney Pollard

Volume 40 (Marxian Economics Section)
THE STATE AND THE ECONOMY UNDER CAPITALISM
by Adam Przeworski

Volume 41 (Theory of the Firm and Industrial Organization Section)
BARRIERS TO ENTRY AND STRATEGIC COMPETITION
by Paul Geroski, Richard J. Gilbert, and Alexis Jacquemin

Volume 42 (Macroeconomic Theory Section)
REDUCED FORMS OF RATIONAL EXPECTATIONS MODELS
by Laurence Broze, Christian Gouriéroux, and Ariane Szafarz

Further titles in preparation
ISSN: 0191-1708